IN QUEST OF
THE INDESCRIBABLE
The Artistry and Life of a Gem Carver

Printed in the United Kingdom

First Edition

ISBN 978-0-9956839-0-7

Please direct all enquiries to:
Gemporia Ltd,
Unit 2D Eagle Road,
Moons Moat,
Redditch,
B98 9HF

www.gemporia.com

Published by: Gemporia Ltd

Book Design: Dan Morris
Front Cover Photo: Ashley Pearson
Back Cover Photo: Tino Hammid

About The Back Cover: A 4.02ct Montana Golden Sapphire TorusRing, with an 82.16ct African Blue Chalcedony carving and a 124.49ct Black Drusy Agate carving. **AGTA 1998 Cutting Edge Award Winner and DM 500 Prize Honorable Mention.** One of two foreign entries to win, for the first time, the German Carvers and Engravers Association Award. All the pieces are held together by carved stone in the tongue and groove technique, without metal or adhesives. With the turn of a stone knob on the back, all the pieces come about.

IN QUEST OF THE INDESCRIBABLE

The Artistry and Life of a Gem Carver

The story and journey that led me to the far reaches of this planet, the deepest core of an atom, all the while guiding my soul and spirit in a lifelong quest in Art, Science and Enlightenment.

by Glenn Lehrer, G.G.

Dedication

This book is dedicated to my loving wife of 36 years, Sharon, who recognized my talent before I even knew I was that good. All these years she has remained my best friend, lover and co-business partner. I would not be writing this book without her being there always in co-partnership, for most of my living days on this Earth.

FOREWORD

Steve Bennett, CEO, Gemporia

It took me a while to get Glenn to agree to write this book, but I was persistent to a point of becoming really annoying with my buddy. But why? Well, I have spent many an hour with Glenn over the past five years and I don't think I can name a single hour where I haven't learned something. His knowledge of crystallography, gemology, geology, mineralogy and all things science seems never ending. Admittedly I dropped out of school, so you could argue that even someone teaching me my times tables might be of educational benefit to me! And quite frankly you would have a valid point. However, whilst I am not well read on many things, I have for many years eagerly studied gemstones. So normally, I can do a reasonably good job of holding my own when it comes to discussing my chosen subject. But with Glenn, I have learned to embrace the saying, "You have two ears and one mouth, so use them accordingly".

I really wanted Glenn to write this book for several reasons. One of course was that I knew many of my customers would love to discover more about the man behind the fabulous TorusRing cut. I have always maintained the more you learn about the gems you acquire, the more you enjoy them. But for me, the key reason was Glenn's unparalleled views and incredibly deep knowledge in crystallography. I had once witnessed Glenn put glass models of the 7 different crystal systems in front of a dozen or so of our TV presenters and key management team and ask them to pick which shape appealed to them the most. Then I sat back in amazement, as he went on to accurately describe each of their individual personality traits. I am sure all readers will be amazed by the section on crystallography, as it explains why we get drawn to certain gemstones.

Steve Bennett, November 2016

SPECIAL THANKS

To my mother Ruth, who did not always like what I did or places I went in the world, but always supported and encouraged me to venture out into the world and explore with freedom. She would always tell me to do what was right for me and not worry what the world expects of you. She taught me and supported me to follow my own passion and interests, not necessarily what society expected of me. This was my key to learning, to find freedom with responsibility. Mother is 101 years old and what I believe has been a big key to her longevity is she always adapted to change and she was always learning and exploring new things and areas of interest in her life. Always growing and open to the new. These two key principles I have absorbed and integrated into my life.

To my older brother Wayne, who back in 1975 placed that polished cut piece of optical Quartz in my hand that started the journey that has led to a lifetime of adventure. Your genius has always been to see beyond life's limitations to a virgin future. And as my older brother, growing up you always looked out for me and was always gracious enough to allow me to tag along with the "older boys." Thus taking me places beyond what my age normally might call appropriate. We have had adventures growing up that have been a thread of understanding throughout my life.

To my late father, who lived to be 92 years old. He taught me by example and word that if you get knocked down, you pick yourself up, dust yourself off and persist. Don't let life's hard edges ever stop you from your purpose or focus. The most successful people in life fail several times, but when they succeed, they excel. Throughout my career I've hit many hard walls and many upsets but never seemed to get, or stay, depressed. I will have buckled down, focused and re-invented myself several times in my 40-year career. I have you, Dad, to thank for this in the way you raised me to stand independently on my own two feet.

To Lawrence Stoller who so many years ago knocked on my door, asking if I'd teach him how to cut a crystal. He became my first student, who quickly morphed into a co-creative partner. MegaGems was born from our partnership as well as a lifelong true good friend and brother. Together we created some of the most incredible Gem Art two artists could create as one. We mapped out how two individual artists can come together and co-create and innovate in our industry, changing the mindset as to what can be done to these ancient large crystals. Also, besides being a long time true friend, you have been a mentor where I know I'm greater because of what I've learned from you over these 34 years of friendship and co-creativity par excellence.

To my spiritual teachers who helped at critical times to lead me out of deep dark tunnels. Seen and unseen, who helped illuminate the light at the end of the tunnel for me to focus, learn and grow through all these many years: there are many of you, but I'd like to acknowledge the two most significant in my life.

First, the late Angeles Arrien, PhD., a cross-cultural anthropologist with Basque heritage and a fully trained Vision Maker in her culture. The term is used in the Basque culture to refer to the Community Elder who knows of the seen and unseen worlds, has passed the necessary initiations and is acknowledged as an elder wise one of her culture. You were the one who taught me, "To walk the spiritual path with practical feet".

Second, Lazaris and Jach Purcel. From the moment I heard you live on Sept 23, 1979 in Marin County, my life has forever changed so much because of your guidance and true friendship. After all these years, your words and wisdom have always rung true for me. You have helped in ways beyond words for me to find my way back home, to realize true enlightenment by living from a place of freedom with responsibility. Finally coming to the place where true enlightenment in oneself is not the end but the beginning. I am forever grateful for your mentorship and loving friendship. You will find many quotes from Lazaris throughout this book.

I need to really acknowledge Si and Ann Fraizer, without whom I believe I would not have been placed on the map of gem carving, were it not for the many articles they wrote about my work for Lapidary Journal. Si and Ann are one of those rare couples that are so passionate about Gem Art. Because of Si and Ann, my work has been seen worldwide in the many magazines articles written about my pieces. I am forever indebted to the two of them. Thank you both.

There are many others whom I know I should thank but the list would be just too long. You know who you are. But to name a few, I wish to thank Bill Larson from Pala International who has always supported and collected my work and was instrumental in helping to get Bahia into the GIA. Edward Boehm from Rare Source, who was instrumental in getting

Bahia to be placed permanently at the GIA. And Bill Boyajian, my GIA colored gemstone instructor and past president of the GIA who really helped light the fire in my belly for the science of gemology. And his ultimate gift to me, as president at the time, for having the GIA acquire the Bahia sculpture for permanent exhibition at their world campus in Carlsbad, California.

I also wish to acknowledge some of my past and present apprentices. I could not have done what I did without them. No artist can do it all alone and without dedicated individuals who want to learn the craft, artists like myself could not have achieved the degree of success without them. Sean Davis, whose abilities as a student apprentice and eventually a master in the craft of gem carving in his own right, helped launch my career in those early years. Somdee Chanthrapat, who was forever there for me as a skilled lapidarist and would accompany me to Bangkok, Thailand when we set up one of my first studios outside the US. And finally Aaron Sangenitto, who currently is studying and working alongside of me as an apprentice as we speak. Your attention to detail is one of your greatest gifts. Your artistic skill is in and of itself amazing.

And last but not least to my very good friend and co-venture partner, Steve Bennett from Gemporia for believing and seeing in me my talent as a hidden gem that could be brought to the larger world of gemstone and jewelry lovers, beyond the small circle of gemstone miners, gem dealers and jewelry designers. I would not be writing this book if it was not for you. Steve, you have opened tangible horizons that were only dreams and visions of my future. To me you are the living embodiment of consciously creating success, all the while having fun. These qualities and principles I personally admire in another. You have been a true mentor of genius in so many ways for me. The Thais have a saying, "If it's not fun, it's not good business." Steve, you are a 21st century mapmaker in the artistry of business and commerce. You live it with integrity and unending creativity. You have helped me in ways I will be eternally grateful for.

CONTENTS

PRELUDE

"Live the life you've imagined."
Henry David Thoreau (1817-1892)

How does one write about oneself and about one's own art form without coming across pompous, arrogant or removed from the larger world? The opportunity to write a book did, at first glance, come to me as a real challenge. I struggled for months to find the motivation or clarity as to what to write about. When my good friend and co-venture partner Steve Bennett of Gemporia asked me to write a book about myself for his customers, I found I had tremendous resistance to beginning the process. I had to ask Steve, "What should I write about, other than a book with lots of pretty pictures of my work?" His reply was, "Part education, travels and adventures to remote places in the world, along with a general interest in gemstones and gemology in your own words. And of course, lots of pictures."

It has always been easy for me to get up in front of a crowd and show slides of my work, and to share the process of creating my art along with telling adventure gemstone stories. After all my wife, Sharon, is always telling me what a great storyteller I am and how fascinating my adventures are. Of course, I had always planned to do a coffee-table style book of my art sometime in the future. Sometime way off in the future. Never in my life did I consider writing a memoir as a gemstone artist before Steve Bennett asked me to. To write a book about myself almost seemed vain, a bit arrogant even, I thought. And even then, it became an off and on process searching for my voice in the written word.

As an individual and artist, I have been working hard in most of my adult years to mitigate my arrogance, especially about being an artist. I have spent years working hard learning to be a 'normal', natural type of person beyond airs and 'better than' attitude. I've learned, sometimes by challenging experiences as I've grown older, to show more gratitude for those around me and in life in general. And especially not to come across as an arrogant, struggling artist who believed the world owed me something. To write a book about myself pushed me right up against this very edge.

For years, I have enjoyed the luxury of others writing stories and covering the many different levels of my art and accomplishments in the trade press magazines, magazine covers, published books, live lectures and on live network television. There is a vast collection of articles and books that have been written about me if the reader wishes to follow up on my work. As they now say, "Just Google me".

At first thought, given an opportunity to write one's own memoir seemed a bit premature. At the moment I see my art just beginning to take on a whole new dimension, drawing on the previous 38 years. How could I write a memoir when I feel I've only lived half to two-thirds of the story so far?

After great consideration and a few 'aha!' moments, I realized what a fantastic opportunity it is to share with the world the life, art and inside view of a Gem Artist's mind and studio. Plus, to be able to share with fans of my art the real adventure behind the story of becoming a Gem Artist. The world of gems has, for centuries, seemed shrouded in perpetual secrecy. The opportunity to put down in print for others to read the true, very personal story and journey that led me to being a Gem Artist began to excite me.

The secrets of the gem trade have been held very closely for centuries. I have come to see this book as a rare opportunity to create a descriptive picture of gem cutting and carving by throwing open a wide door to my world of business and art, to those lovers of gems who would never normally be shown the sourcing and creating of this rarefied art form. A form perhaps more shrouded in obscurity than even the alchemist formula to turn lead into gold! To delve deep into the inner most nature of our world that I am forever contemplating is a never-ending passion of mine. It has also been my quest and destiny as a conscious spiritual being to unite the world of the seen with the worlds of the unseen. Gemstone Artistry became, and still is, my passion - a way to blend these two paradoxical worlds. It is not just about my art but about the inner core of our quest as humans to know and understand the very nature of our being and the planet we call home. My art has always been the avenue where I felt I could fuse this ancient knowledge of, "As Above, So Below" - the vehicle for my quest for self-realization.

As humans, we have always been seeking to feel part of this greater place called Earth. Belonging is one of the most primordial drives in our DNA, fugitively speaking. Where all life seeks to find order out of chaos. To fulfill one's destiny through understanding and experience of greater states of consciousness as we live our lives. The very molecular nature of crystallized gemstones stand as sentinels in this very evolutionary drive to higher states of complexity and intelligence. As humans, to be able to contribute to our world and feel we are living our destiny through individual accomplishments, complex relationships and sentinel achievements is the very drive built into all life and our universe. You might say it is the very evolutionary path all molecular life is on. To feel we are leaving this world a better place than how we first encountered it seems to me to be a driving natural principle of a very high order. To find and live one's true destiny in a lifetime is a strong fulfillment that many of us seem to desire.

I hope in a small way this book becomes a window to these deeper states of understanding, thus augmenting one's personal and global awareness of the planet in this vast universe we call home. To ignite in the reader a deeper sense of passion, imaginations and in a small way to light a spark of desire to reach greater heights in oneself. To inspire the reader to find and explore the inner Genius that lays within every one of us on this planet. My intention is to share with you my journey of understanding as seen through the mineral kingdom and the living of life to one's fullest. A lifelong quest for enlightenment through my art, science and spirituality.

And of course, lots of pretty pictures of my Gem Art!

1

INTRODUCTION

"Function always precedes form".
(This is also a basic concept in architecture.)
Lazaris

*"Success or luck, is where preparation meets opportunity.
The key is the ability to seize the moment."*
Steve Bennett

This is the story of how I grew up to be a Gem Artist, and the journey that led me on the adventure of a lifetime.

My journey into the world of gems and minerals began in the most unusual way. It did not come from family or an obvious aptitude for the sciences of natural history during my formative years growing up. Nor from an opportunity that came my way during my early twenties from being "in the business" or finding a teacher to apprentice with. No one in my family, that I am aware of, was into jewelry or gemstones. My father was a Stock Investment Manager and my mother a working business woman in management during the 1950s and 1960s while I was growing up. Becoming a Gem Artist was not even a straight line to where I would find my creative profession and passion for the next 38 years. Starting out, there were no teachers to study under in America, or at least that I was aware of. Finding my destiny is definitely not the way most would think or imagine that I became interested in gemstones. I did not even know such an art form existed back when I was a child and adolescent.

I will start out by sharing a very intimate selection of stories and mystical experiences that opened my mind to a much larger universe that I had no understanding or knowledge of at the time. These unique and mysterious experiences have proven to be the very nucleus to the understanding of my unceasing and ever deepening reflection of the complexity of this universe. My love for Gem Art has become the lens that takes these rarified natural gemstones and beams light, beauty, love and imagination out into the world. This is my quest to capture this indescribable art in a lasting and enduring presence for generations to hold, marvel and be inspired by.

The story I am about to tell you takes you on the journey of how I discovered my muse in Gem Art, through the places I've traveled, the interesting and exotic people I've met along the way, individuals I've learned from, the diverse cultures I've encountered and significant events that occurred in my life. Discovering the many pieces of the puzzle that have interconnected everything into a synergy that has propelled me for several decades of passionate pursuit. Where the whole of my life is greater than the sum of the parts.

I will share, through my own understanding as a gemologist, the world of mineralogy and crystallography that gives deeper understanding and credence to my story.

I will open up the doors of my studio and share with you the art, the tools and techniques I have invented, learned and explored to be able to create the beauty that is required to execute gemstone carving. This is the sanctum where the magic happens and where historically the doors are normally closed to the larger world, the inner chambers where I drop deep into an altered state and experience over and over again the brilliance of the light that shines in every gemstone that is birthed in my studio.

This book is my story, where the mysteries of the universe converse through the natural rare beauty of the mineral kingdom, a kingdom that connects us to the very core of an atom and simultaneously to the farthest reaches of deep space. I have come to call this the "Big History." It is a piece of this timeless knowledge and wisdom that I feel I fuse into every finished gemstone that flows from my hands. I hope to paint a story for the reader of what lies behind or within each gemstone creation and out into this world. One could say the very course of my life's journey is alchemically woven into every gemstone I carve or cut. I can clearly see this now. You might suggest I know I'm fulfilling my personal destiny and giving to a greater purpose of humanity as a whole.

The book is not written in chronological order. It's a memoir with stories and chapters that lay a foundation for my awakening as a Gem Artist in the order I felt best expresses my coming of age as a Gem Artist. It is written like a story of the hero's journey, as I come of age and mature in my field of expertise and life in its wholeness. You could say I jumped backwards and forwards in time, as I laid the chapters out to build a foundation of all the parts of my life, crystallizing in some form of synergy. The order to the chapters is the foundation to why I am a Gem Artist.

In some of the chapters I repeat myself two or three times around the same experience or piece of knowledge that I hold of importance. In my own levels of comprehending I know I often need to hear something at least three times. There is a power in repeating an important point or fact, each time it can sink deeper, creating a greater sense comprehension and visualization. In certain chapters, such as Chapter 14 on crystallography and Chapter 7 on tools and techniques, I felt by repeating myself the layperson, who maybe hearing it for the first time, can begin to comprehend.

This book will take you on a journey, where I'm hoping to mold the reader into a uniformity paralleled with a reflection of beauty and inspiration. It is where science and art merge to create a synergy that is greater than the sum of its parts because of this co-relationship. To me, Gem Art is a powerful medium that best embodies the ancient archetypal Greek Goddess Muse. It is my mainline to the Goddess where all life emerges out of, so God can shine in the minds of humanity. This is the deeper meaning of what the Ancient Greeks meant when they empowered the Goddess Muse as the archetype of the true blend of science and art. It is in my chosen muse where the knowledge of science and the beauty of art itself blends, creating a profound lasting powerful vessel of wonder and imagination that can last generations.

2

THE JOURNEY TO THE CORE OF AN ATOM

· How It All Began
· The Dramatic Introduction to the Sublime

My adventure into the world of gems and crystal began in 1975 just after I had returned from traveling, when my brother, Wayne, handed me a cut and polished Quartz crystal. As I held the crystal, I felt a surge of energy run from my hand, up through my arm and explode in my head. It was like a bolt of lightning exploding throughout my mind and body. Never before had I felt anything so powerful, let alone from a physical inanimate object. It was the early 70s and the world of crystals, their energy and beauty, wasn't yet in the public awareness. I knew nothing about minerals and crystal at the time. I had no interest in jewelry.

I had just returned home from traveling the world for two and a half years without a clue in my mid-twenties as to what to do with my life. Prior to returning home, I was in search of meaning to my life after dropping out of college after just the first year. During some of this time I lived in a very remote monastery in Southern India as a Yogi in daily mediation and ritual, searching for meaning and inner peace, leaving behind my Western occidental upbringing.

It was this single cut piece of Quartz crystal so many years back that was handed to me, that intrigued me enough to go out and buy my first pieces of lapidary equipment. I started to teach myself how to cut. This evolved into a lifelong profession. At the time, I had no clue that an art form like this existed. I was completely naive to the world of gems as an artistic expression. There were no schools or teachers that I could enroll with to begin an apprenticeship. I was on my own, learning and exploring, with no idea where this would take me. I was working outside a box I did not even know existed at the time - I was following an inner calling, diving deep into my passion as an artist, only wanting to explore this intriguing medium. In some unconscious sense there laid a treasure waiting to be discovered. I had to begin the journey - and let the road lead me one footstep at a time.

Later in the book I will share my understanding and knowledge of what I felt on that day when my brother handed me the Quartz crystal. I will go into greater depth how our consciousness is a mirror of the very symmetry of the mineral kingdom, which forms with exacting crystallography. So much has been thrown around these last three decades in New Age circles about crystal power and gemstone energy. I will share my 40 years' exploration and study of the symmetry of crystals in nature and the corresponding symmetry of our consciousness. We live our lives constantly seeking or creating order and symmetry, just like in nature. The smallest atom is driven in the same way that we as humans structure our lives to find order and symmetry. I developed a tool and have tested it with hundreds of individuals which explains this simple but deep understanding of resonance. My understanding comes from both my spiritual experiences and a deeply grounded knowledge of the science of mineralogy and crystallography. Together they paint the bigger picture of self-awareness. You could say you see your reflection in the light of refraction. But I need to back up a bit here to tell you where it actually all started, even before my brother handed me this cut piece of optical Quartz in back in 1975. One would assume this is how the story all began but the real journey started five years earlier at the age of 18.

It began when I started having a series of paranormal, mystical and out-of-body experiences. At the time I didn't know anything about this. It was completely foreign and abstract when it started to happen to me. All I knew was that I began to have spontaneous, natural, non-drug aided experiences that felt so divine and ecstatic I could not deny the power of them. I was raised in an atheist, Jewish family with no formal religious upbringing. What started in my late teens with these very real mystical experiences, became the core, the knowledge, the enlightenment and the very inspiration from which I eventually discovered my muse in Gem Art.

During this time, when I was having these recurring, totally natural and spontaneous paranormal experiences, I was led on a spiritual journey that took me to the very core of the atom in our universe and the far reaches of our planet, towards answers to these perplexing experiences.

I spontaneously began to have what might be termed as out-of-body or astral projection experiences, in part some form of Eastern practices often associated with these types of altered states of consciousness. In the beginning of these very profound experiences I had no real knowledge or basis for what was happening to me. They just began to occur, emerging at night from my lucid dream states.

It is here where my story of becoming a Gem Artist truly begins. I will share a few intimate stories for the first time in public so as to connect the dots of how it all began for me. How my muse awoke in these deeper states of awareness, merging together my creative, artistic urge to create with my soul's search for a deeper meaning to life. How these very supernatural experiences led me to find my true expression of art that I would come to find as my medium of expression in this lifetime. As beginnings go, this is really where it all began for me.

Out of these very real paranormal experiences came the understanding of the core of the physics and chemistry of our universe. As a child I was not into or good at science and math. I was mediocre in school when it came to academics. I spent most of my time surfing Californian waves (not internet surfing!) and enjoying art classes in school. Science was the farthest thing from my interest growing up. These deeper states of consciousness woke me up to the genius that lies in each and every one of us. These experiences have, over the following decades of my life, revealed how real and truly enlightening these heightened moments are in my life. This is why I like to call it the "Big Reality", versus the physical reality we are familiar with in our everyday life.

When I returned to college to study Earth Sciences, Mathematics and Chemistry seven years later, I was able to validate these paranormal experience as the truth of our known universe. I knew they were real beyond theory, as my professors were lecturing and postulating, more real than the very physical world we tend to call 'reality'. Here is where I felt the complete confirmation that what I had experienced in these altered states was an amazing fact that science was putting forth, as what we now understand of the atomic and cosmic world to be true.

As I define it, the "Big Reality" is hidden inside everything we call the physical dimension or world. I have come to merge my esoteric and scientific understanding of these dimensions with my chosen field of art. For the first time ever in print, since my first awakening 42 years ago, I will share these very personal and intimate experiences that I have not spoken of publicly until now. I'm about to share how these paranormal experiences began and ultimately guided me to Gem Art as my chosen path in life.

You may wonder what this mystical world has to do with Gem Art and my life as a lapidarist and jewelry designer? In fact, it has everything to do with my art. It has been my inspiration and moral compass throughout my life. In the following paragraphs, I will share some of these extraordinary experiences and how they have had a profound impact on my artistry and my living of life. Whether you follow a particular religious faith or not, the stories I am about to share will give insight to a world beyond the physical. Worlds more real than the physical dimension we seem to make so real. This is the "Big Reality" that I have coined that has motivated me in my art, the true beginning into the world of mystery.

At the age of 18 I began to have these spontaneous outer body states of awareness and mystical experiences that led me to the very core of an atom, and to the far reaches of this planet in search of answers that my Western upbringing could not answer. This is at the root of my search and my lifelong quest of this indescribable, sublime world of the mystical. It has been my primary focus throughout my life. Along with these mystical journeys in out-of-body states I also began to have psychic audio recognition where I could hear others' thoughts and feelings in my head.

Many years ago, this was very frightening. Now they are my inner guides, and have been throughout my adult life. I can see how one can walk that fine line between genius and insanity because at the time my society gave no value to these deeper states of consciousness. It was not until I began to explore Eastern mysticism that I found some form of comfort and understanding that I was not insane but was having profound experiences that mystics, monks and students of Eastern thought would seek all their life. For me, that happened without seeking or desiring them to occur. My seeking was to look for the answers and understandings as to what these mystical experiences meant.

So, back to where it all started one night at the age of 18. It began with a very vivid, lucid dream. In this dream, I remember standing on a diving board at a swimming pool and jumping into the water. I dove deep under water into the deep end of a pool. For me, water has always been my element from a young age and into my teens as a surfer growing up in California. At first it seemed completely natural and just an ordinary dream when it began. But when I attempted to reach the surface, I struggled to get my head above the water. The surface of the water never seemed to be there. The more I struggled to reach the top the further it appeared to be. In the beginning of these recurring dreams I would eventually awake, choking as though I had almost drowned. Following this first night, the dream kept happening in exactly the same way, night after night. Diving into the water, going deep, struggling to reach the surface, waking from the dream gasping for air. I kept having these recurring, very real dreams, gasping for air only to wake in fear that I was drowning.

On about the fifth night of this recurring dream, while under water (again and again still trying to reach the surface with to avail) a voice inside my head spoke as clear as day, "Relax and just breathe". Breathe under water, how is this possible I thought? At first, I doubted this voice that spoke out of nowhere. Somehow, eventually trusting the voice in the dream, I threw my arms back, relaxed and just began to breathe under water as though I was breathing air.

What happened next is, to this day, one of the most profound experiences I have ever had in my life, let alone in a night dream. As soon as I relaxed and began breathing normally as though I was taking in air, this very load roaring sound, like a locomotive train in a tunnel, started rumbling in my head. It became louder and louder in my mind until a giant explosion went off in my brain and a supernova of lights filled my mind's eye. It was the most ecstatic, blissful experience I had ever experienced. I felt this most incredible rapture. I later came to understand these happenings as what Eastern Mysticism calls Nirvana. In Western esoterica, one could call it a rapture state of being taken up by God. It is so difficult to find the right words to express this most pleasurable, blissful, other-worldly experience.

If one is unfamiliar with the term "out-of-body experience", it is not a dream state but where one's consciousness lifts from their physical body and can travel to any place on the planet or to dimensions beyond this physical world often not hindered by space nor time. At least not space or time as we think of it in physical terms apply here. These realms have been described as astral, casual and ethereal realms of consciousness. Many indigenous people around the world have spoken of this realm or state of being as the spirit world where one can travel in a conscious or unconscious dream-like state.

There were times when I would have an out-of-body experience where I would lift out of my physical body, look back at my sleeping body in bed, get up and walk right through a physical wall in into the garden of my home I was living in at the time. Everything was there just like it was physically solid, but instead I could see the space between molecules and walk right through what appears as solid state. There are no boundaries with regards to physicality when one is in this astral state. One can actually see the light glow from this space in molecules and atoms. It is truly a mystical experience.

For several nights following this initial awakening I would go through this ritual of lying down, begin to feel like I was falling asleep, no longer needing to go through the underwater experience. The process would repeat itself, starting with hearing a roaring locomotive thundering sound in my head, followed by an explosion of myriad blinding lights. I found myself in some other world, universe or dimension each time. This blissful, ecstatic experience of seeing beyond the physical is what I now believe could be called a God experience, although it is not associated with any particular religion or spiritual teaching or dogma of any type. I felt truly at home and at one with "God, Goddess, All There Is" or in the realm of '"Divine Memory", as one of my spiritual teachers, Lazaris, describes this state of being as. Having these ultimate experiences are what many throughout the ages of time have sought. For me, experiencing these rapture states became the path to my Higher Self, and God, Goddess and Enlightenment. Looking back now I can see how by going through the chaos, I found a sublime order in symmetry and dimension to our world and myself of what I call "crystallinity".

Crystallinity refers to the degree of structural order in a solid. In a crystal, the atoms or molecules are arranged in a regular, periodic symmetrical manner. The degree of crystallinity has a big influence on hardness, density, transparency and diffusion in a mineral and most gemstones. Compare this to a gas, where the relative positions of the atoms or molecules are completely random without an order or structure. In our lives we often refer to the degree of transparency: if one can feel and communicate it, there is order to a thought, idea, company, society etc. Chaos on the human level is seen as change on a personal and global level. The beauty of understanding crystal structure in nature is being able to see how we as humans organize our thoughts, knowledge, relationships, family and society in symmetrical patterns.

The Mystical Experience That Was the Initial Doorway to My Future Self

These ecstatic experiences were many and varied but one in particular proved to be the most significant towards my future artist expression in Gem Art, long before I knew this is what

I wanted do with my life or knew the art form even existed. It was also these mystical experiences that led me back to college to study mineralogy and gemology a few years later. I had a burning drive inside my soul to fuse the mystical, the beauty of art and the knowledge of science blending as one state of wholeness. You might say in my own way "a unified theory of everything seen and unseen".

During one of my out-of-body experiences I found myself traveling through what seemed to be outer space with a ball of light that was a Being of intelligence.

I say intelligent because though they had no recognizable physical form, its orb of brilliant lights possessed an amazing intelligence. We were communicating with one another without verbal word but only within our minds at lightning speed. It was bodies of vast information and an accurate comprehensive body of knowledge in what seemed like nanoseconds of time. In other words, neither this light being nor myself had a physically recognizable body. We were both orbs of light and consciousness flying through space at what felt like immense speeds. He or she, for there was no sex associated to our forms, were able to communicate with one another in complete whole streams of thought in quick rapid fire seconds. In modern digital terms I was being downloaded with vast complex systems of thought in what is comparable to a single push of a button.

As we flew through space I could see other pairs of orbs of conscious light traveling in every direction in space. I asked my guide of light where all these individuals were going. Their answer was: to different realms throughout the universe to learn and study.

They then communicated to me that we were headed to a very direct and specific place in the universe for my specific purpose. When we reached our destination, I found myself in an electromagnetic energy field. In other words there was no solid visible wall of containment but I could sense and see a field of energy/electricity that created a very defined boundary held together by electromagnetic energy. I could sense the force of the field and see transparent colors that was being reflected by this force field. When I asked the Light Being where was I, the answer was, "You are inside the very core of an atom. What you understand as physical form is only a resonance of energy that casts an image of solid physicality when one is viewing from what is your physical body." How could something be contained without any solid matter? This was completely foreign and new to my understanding. Remember, up to this point when it came to anything remotely scientific I felt I was a complete Neanderthal and had no real education in the physics of atom. But yet in this instant I totally conceived and understood the depth of this knowledge of what New Physics was theorizing. I totally got the truth of this experience in this mystical state as a real truth to our universe.

Several years later when I returned to college to study mineralogy, crystallography and physics to understand the medium of gemstones as my art form I found myself hearing my chemistry professor say, "99.9999% of an atom is space and even there is doubt anything is solid about an atom in the 0.0001% we don't know yet." He was speaking about a theory, but I had an amazing realization that for me it was a very real experience, when I reflected back to this paranormal experience seven years earlier. This was one of the many true validations that my mystical experiences were more real and not some pipe dream, fantasy experience or illusion of a crazy person. It is the very essence of this realization that "form follows function". All life is composed of resonant energy that downsteps down to a physical form and appears concrete in our minds while you are in physical form.

At about the same time, other mystical, unexplainable experiences were occurring in my life. For instance, I was able to hear voices that were not spoken orally but only heard within my mind. You might say that could be confused with the mind of a person gone insane. I often contemplate this thin fine line between prophetic and insane. I've come to know this mystical experience as "Oral Audio Transmission".

When I'd be talking to friends I'd hear what they were thinking or feeling - but then I would realize they weren't speaking out loud. Initially I thought they were actually speaking to me, but when I realized they weren't speaking out loud and yet I was hearing their thoughts and feelings in my head, I was scared. At first, when I thought I was hearing them speak I'd respond to them from what I heard in thought and feeling and not the spoken word. Well, you can imagine the look that would come over their faces. "How did you know this?" Fear would set in and they would quickly find a way to leave me, afraid that I had a power over them or was doing something to them.

As a result, I began to feel alienated. My friends didn't want to be around me. They thought I was some evil person who was into mind control. This was not what I was about, but since I didn't fully understand what was happening to me, I chose to remove and isolate myself from my friends as a way to avoid these awkward situations. It took a while for me to realize what was actually happening to me and I began to learn to shield myself from others' thoughts so I would not invade their space or be inundated by their thoughts and feelings.

I tell this because I also feel gemstones in their rough state talk to me. Not like a human verbal voice but a wisdom or knowledge as to what I should do to make the most of this precious piece of Earth. And I'm not the only gem cutter who talks like this. It seems more often than not a Gem Artist will explain how stones talk to them. These precious natural rough gem pieces guide me to do the right thing. When I begin, they tell me things about themselves and a co-creative process of cutting and carving with them. I have an ability to hear beyond the physical realm which I now put to positive use in my work. Later in the book I will explain more about how minerals communicate to me and how I co-create with each gem piece I carve.

Oral Transmission with the Fool on the Hill in Istanbul

One most memorable stories of my "oral transmission" happened during my travels around the world. I will go into more detail about my travels in the next chapter, but the below experiences expand more on how I grew to understand and embrace this oral audio transmission, and so seems key here.

I had just flown from Greece to Turkey and was dramatically confronted with the difference between the Western, Occidental culture that I grew up in, and the Asian, Oriental culture of the East that I had just stepped into. Turkey was so amazing and so different from anything I'd ever experienced whilst growing up in Los Angeles.

I was with a group of young American men. They all wanted to go to the brothels in Istanbul - the brothel they chose was a giant, four-square block neighborhood with a big wall surrounding it and a big gate to walk through.

I had never in my life seen anything like this nor had I ever gone to a brothel. I went in, curious to see what a brothel was like: the women were dressed in lingerie sitting in a living room with a large picture window facing the street. You walk down the street window shopping until you find the one you want to have sex with. I found myself totally repulsed by the place, so I decided to leave my friends behind.

As I sat outside the large entry gate, I noticed a man cooking a shish kabob of lamb on a skewer over a small charcoal burner. The man appeared to be making his living cooking and selling to the men who were hungry after having sex. He had a serene, calm, peaceful look on his face. As I watched him a thought crossed my mind, "This was the "wise fool on the hill". Just as I had this thought he looked up, stared straight at me from a hundred feet away, smiled and shook his head in agreement with a wide grin on his face. This guy heard my thoughts. In my head I heard, "Yes, you are right, I come here nightly to watch this debauchery and make my living selling them my BBQ lamb." Then at this moment a huge smile crossed both of our faces. We both had a completely silent but oral transmission - we spoke to one another in our minds beyond physical words.

From my studies with my Sufi teacher in college, I had learned that a true spiritual teacher often passes on their wisdom and knowledge to their student by internal, non-verbal transmission, not by books or lecture. This was one of those moments. I communicated with a stranger non-verbally and he communicated to me from a non-verbal place. We knew what each other was thinking and we acknowledged that to each other.

How the Mystical Meets the Physical

I had made my way to the south of India after three months traveling overland from Istanbul. I had arrived at the land of mysticism and spirituality. I took up the life of a wondering mystic - I knew there was more to life than my Western Los Angeles, Judeo-Christian, non-religious upbringing that seemed to me to be completely entrapped in the materialism of life. I just needed to move outside the box of the Western collective to find it. I would say in my wanderings, "I am a leaf in the wind, letting each day or person point me in the next direction to go on my travels". It was a complete state of "freedom without responsibility." I began a journey going from place to place with no specific agenda. I stepped over this imaginary line between the Western/Occidental view of the world and into the mystical, Eastern philosophy of life, reincarnation and karma. Into a mystical land with a history of over 10,000 years, I was enthralled and enchanted. I felt so free. I was beginning to feel some form of connection to this surreal reality I was experiencing in altered states.

I was walking and wandering down the South Eastern coast of India, known for its ancient temples and palaces. I walked and hitchhiked from ancient temple to ancient temple during the day and from ashram to ashram at night. It had been over six months since I left behind my world in America and was now here half way around the world and miles apart in culture.

I arrived on the southern Indian town of Pondicherry where the famous Sri Aurobindo ashram was founded and established by the late yogi Aurobindo. There are ashrams scattered all over India and for the most part they are open and free to stay at during this period for anyone who is looking for spiritual refuge. At many of these ashrams I was often given a dormitory bed to sleep in, one hot meal a day and the opportunity to participate in the meditation, chanting and spiritual practice of the ashram. I was completely free and there was no pressure to have to belong to a particular group. Life in India is amazing this way. Completely tolerant of the many religions and cultures that have come and merged on its continent over its very long history. Each person is given complete freedom to feel and choose his or her path of devotion.

The first night there I had another profound dream and altered state of consciousness. In this particular dream an old Indian man with a white beard appeared in my dream, dressed in rags and a white bandana-like turban. I had no idea who he was. All I could feel was this person had a profound and powerful presence. He approached me in the dream and with one of his hands he touched the crown of my head. I felt this loud roaring, rushing sound and energy in my whole body crescendo into the most ecstatic state of Love I have ever felt – it filled me with lights and color. I call it the divine state of Love. It was bliss beyond words.

I awoke the next morning still feeling this afterglow of sheer ecstasy. It was truly a very profound, lucid dream lying in the afterglow. Deciding I needed to take a walk and stroll down the street to let the waves of this afterglow settle and process in my mind and heart, I entered the city and began to walk.

As I walked down some small side street, this voice out of nowhere spoke inside my head as clear as day. The voice I had come to recognize spoke so clearly and loudly to me, "Stop, look to the right and go into that shop". As I looked to my right I saw a small, Indian style sacred jewelry shop. They often contained the many small statues of deities from Hindu and Buddhist traditions. They would have pictures and small enamel medallions of saints and popular deities. Having learned to listen to this inner voice I turned and walked into the shop. I looked down into the jewelry case and to my amazement there was a medallion of that bearded Indian I dreamt of the night before. I was stunned. I asked the shopkeeper, "Who is this man or saint?" All he could say was, "He was no ordinary man, this is Shirdi Sai Baba, a Sufi saint who lived at the turn of the 19th into the 20th century."

The story is no one knew who this holy man Shirdi Sai Baba was or where he had come from. He just turned up one day in the town of Shirdi and began to perform miracles for the locals. Here it was: I dreamt of this guy who lived almost 100 years ago, a saint in India I'd never heard of who came to me in a dream, and through his presence I'd experienced this profound sense of ecstatic, Divine Love. Wow, this was another one of those mystical, non-physical experiences that felt more real than physical: a paradox to me. My life was beginning to blend between the physical and ethereal realms, resolving into a single state of being. I was just beginning to find answers to what began in my dream state three years earlier in my late teens.

The story did not end here. To further deepen this experience of who Shirdi Sai Baba was, as I continued my travels in southern India, numerous - and I mean numerous - wondering sadhus, holy monks and yogis in India would walk straight up to me, look me in the eyes and say, "You must go see Sai Baba". Though Shirdi Sai Baba was no longer alive, there was another reincarnation of him called Satya Sai Baba living in Southern India. I continued on my wandering, lived in this remote ashram for another 6 months after this first experience, but eventually went to see what people were saying about this living reincarnation of Sai Baba and if it was true. When I encountered him, I saw with my own eyes: he was no ordinary man. I saw energy around him in lights that I had only seen in these altered states, except now I was seeing it in my waking normal physical state. It is moments like this when the two worlds start to melt into the One.

At this point I will end this chapter of the story, though I continued to have many other monumental moments and experiences in dream and mediation states. I continued to have these Nirvana blissed experiences. Always starting from a lucid dream and not necessarily seeing the form of Sai Baba, I would transcend into heightened moments of bliss or states of deep knowledge of our reality as human beings.

So what does all this have to do with gemstones, minerals and my art? Mystics have said for hundreds of years the physical is the illusion and the ethereal realms of reality are actually the more real. The physical world is a condensing of higher states of energy seen as light and sound to us. I had certainly experienced this through the many out of body experiences. From these deeper mystical experiences and understanding of the mineral kingdom, my passion for Gem Art has been the perfect vehicle to express my deeper drive for perfection. It has remained as fresh and inspiring as the first day my brother handed me that Quartz crystal back so many years ago. It is where I found a powerful medium to express the mysteries of the universe coupled with my emotional and intellectual knowledge and wisdom. I had found the perfect medium to express this "indescribable" state of love and wisdom - the sort I experienced over and over again in the Indian ashram. In every gem carving and gem that I cut, I've interwoven consciously and subconsciously into that piece this deeper knowledge and wisdom.

Gemstones are the perfect realization and archetype on our planet where out of the sheer chaos of fluid fiery magma, the atoms seek a state of balance and harmony with other atoms. When atoms form this powerful bond with another atom, either itself or with a different element that can bond in a relationship, they line up in magnificent 3D symmetry and perfect repeating geometrical pattern. We define this symmetry in the science of minerals as the "Seven Crystal Systems" which is based on an axis of symmetry. Almost every mineral in nature forms within one of these seven distinctive axes of symmetry.

I will go into more later in the book but as it pertains to these strange powerful experiences I was having I want to cover some of the more powerful principles I first learned in these out of body experiences that were later confirmed in my science studies.

Another powerful principle in our universe is, "All life is driven to seek absolute balance and harmony". In science, it is called zero-degree kelvin (-459.67°F or -273.15°C) - also known as total suspended animation. Of course, this is an unobtainable ideal state in physical form. But atoms have an innate drive to find this perfect state of balance and form molecules as the basic building block of the physical universe. But like all life, physical life never reaches perfection but only a state of excellence, thus ever-evolving in our known expanding universe.

Just like atoms, we as humans are always seeking harmony and balance and striving to seek perfection. But perfection is an ideal we never achieve. We only keep reaching greater and greater states of excellence, greater and greater levels of complexity and order. You might say it is the very drive that most humans have to be in a relationship with another person or, with a deeper drive, to seek and find a soul mate in life.

All life throughout the universe comes out of a state of chaos, seeking balance and harmony, bonding together to create magnificent, ever-evolving realities of excellence. It is in our very nature to find this state, called Love, and bond with others in unity and harmony. Gemstones and minerals are the perfect first step towards this state in physical form. One can understand when the mystics say that the physical world is an illusion or just a reflection of higher states of consciousness. So, when I discovered Gem Art as the perfect expression of what I had experienced in these many mystical realms and experiences, I knew I had found a perfect marriage to reflect these nonphysical states I had experienced that profoundly changed my life. I had found the vehicle of expression to describe the indescribable.

Gemstones give back so much to us as humans. We tend to think of them as innate objects of beauty, but in fact they are the very archetype of the universe that conveys and communicates the deeper realities of this universe; that we can hold and cherish. They give more back, more than we can ever fathom. It is no wonder that these magnificent, beautifully, naturally formed objects have held humanity in awe for millennia.

3

GROWING UP IN LA

· A Short History... I Promise

I have been an artist all my life. I feel compelled to share this part of my life because I believe that so much of one's experience, detours on the path and outrageous adventures one is willing to explore, have a way of giving a greater depth to the overall potential in one's life around succeeding and achieving moments of excellence.

I was born and raised in Los Angeles, "City of Angels", during the 50s and 60s. It is the land of sun, surf, ocean, deserts, mountains, giant redwoods, Hollywood, movie stars, earthquakes and the birth of Disneyland. It is a land with majestic coast lines and ocean, grand mountains, one of the lowest deserts on the planet and rolling oak meadows and pastures. It holds almost every different environmental natural land formation found on Earth, all in one state in America. As natural beauty goes, there are few places on this planet that rival it: to have everything within a half day's drive from home is a real privilege. It is often said that ideas or new cultural trends have started in California and have flowed as change all over the United States and eventually around the planet.

So much of what has emerged from lives in California, such as movies and computers, have influenced cultures near and afar. This is what I grew up in: the middle of a very creatively-inspired caldron of culture.

My family lived less than four miles from the Pacific Ocean, perched on a hill with a view of areas called Beverly Hills, Century City, Westwood and Santa Monica Mountains and Ocean. At the time, California had just around 15 million in population, less than half of what it is now. There was still lots of open space, many orange groves and empty beaches. Many would consider this one of the ideal places to grow up in. And in many ways, that is true. You could say we were middle class with many of the perks. My father owned a deep-sea cabin cruiser boat, decked-out with all the fishing gear to catch enough fish to supply dinners during the week at home. The ocean and the Sierra Nevada Mountain range of California was my oyster from the age of 12. I loved to surf, backpack, camp and enjoy open beach fires with friends along the sheer solitude of the Sierra Nevada Mountains where I would do solo Vision Quests into the outback for inner reflection and physical challenge.

In other ways, by my mid-teens I felt that so much of Los Angeles was the land of just image without substance at the time. Looking back, it seems profound for a kid of 16 to be contemplating this. But it was what drove me to flee Los Angeles at 18 years of age. To seek something outside my own myopic world and the collective consciousness I was raised within. Our family never took vacations together outside of the state of California, so I was so motivated to see the rest of the world beyond Los Angeles once I graduated from High School.

Growing up I was just a very average student in mathematics, science and basic scholastic studies in High School. As a matter of fact, I struggled to pass algebra and higher math. I avoided science of any type because I believed it was beyond my comprehension. I took the belief that I was just not that smart when it came to academics. I believed at the time I was just average. My grade point average of 2.0 was the classic average "C" student in school. I constantly struggled to understand the meaning of math and science. I worked so hard just to get a passing grade in these areas all the way through High School. Never in my life at this time did I realize or think I had an aptitude for Natural Science and Math at this time in my life. Later, in my 20s, when I found my calling in gemstones, I realized it was the way it was taught back then. Clearly my mind was there for the knowledge, it was just not taught in a way I could comprehend or find interesting in any way at the time. The science aspect of my profession would come later to me in life.

Where I found my passion, and excelled in my early childhood and teenage years, was art, sports and theater. I demonstrated at an early age the ability to be artistic in several mediums and be above average in most sports I participated in. I was a gymnast from the age of seven and good enough to compete state-wide in competition. I would spend hours every day on the trampoline, flipping and turning in the air. I learned about balance in monition and the elegance and beauty of the physical form. A quality I can see now in the many creations of my carvings and sculptures I have done over the years.

At the age of 12 I entered the theater as a child actor in a small playhouse across the street from 20th Century Fox Studios.

It was a theater in Hollywood where actors would perform to be recognized and discovered. Being a childhood actor I learned to stand up in front of audiences and project my voice and speak and feel natural in front of crowds. I also learned how to take on character roles in a story and live as though I was that person. Reflecting now, I can see how this skill has come to serve me in my life. I lecture, teach and appear on television and in documentaries with a sense of relaxed ease. Getting up in front of a live audience or in front of a television camera feels totally natural and I never seem to feel nervous or anxious doing it. Having this ability has made such a huge difference in my ability to communicate my art and the science behind it. It was one of those skills that became part of a larger whole in my life that has given greater dimension to everything I do. Over the course of my life I have seen skills that I developed earlier in my life feed into a purpose later in my life. I've come to understand the synergy of every event or exploration has fed into a greater whole in becoming a Gem Artist. The synergy of this accomplishment and achievement has augmented the greater purpose of what I do in my life now, even though at the time you can't understand why. It's like pieces of a puzzle forming a greater whole and richer picture of what has become the main purpose and destiny in my life.

At the age of 13, living in California during the 1960s, just a few miles from the Pacific Ocean and the famous Malibu beach, I discovered and completely immersed myself in surfing. Having mastered gymnastics as a child, turning to surfing was a natural transition. I believe, much to my parents' dissatisfaction, I gave up a promising youthful career in gymnastics and became a full-on California surfer during my teen years. Art and surfing were the only two things

I was really interested in - besides girls! It is a unique but challenging sport where balance and grace in motion create a sublime moment of beauty for but just an instant. No two waves are alike, much like snowflakes. So every ride is as unique as a wave. A total experience of a moment of balance in motion. I share this because many of my gem carvings feel like an impressionist reflection of beauty in motion similar to the crescendo of a wave as it crashes on the beach after traveling miles through the ocean.

Beach life in California was like living a dream in my teens. Once my older brother and friends could drive we would cruise the coast seeking waves, camp on the beach with a fire and cook hot dogs on a spike. This was living the life: constantly surrounded by the beauty of the state feeling forever inspired and motivated by the spectacular diverse scenery of California. I see over and over again this motif of a wave and fluid movement in so many of my art pieces.

The main passion and focus in my youth and adolescent years was the exploration in several mediums of fine and graphic art. I explored figure and portrait drawing, painting with oil, graphic arts and photography. When I reflect back as to what had the most impact on me during these years, it was photography in black and white, old school with film and darkroom tricks. I was so into photography that I was the darkroom manager for High School classes. I think that by playing and exploring the subtle shades, light to dark, in photography I can now see how my eye was in training for what is required in gem faceting and carving. Art to me was freedom. Freedom to dream, freedom to explore uninhibited, with few boundaries to restrict my vision. I can now see these formative years as the foundation that would give me endurance when I started down this path as a Gem Artist. I often reflect on how extremely fortunate I was to have grown up in America and specifically California where one has complete freedom to explore their passion and express themselves as individuals. My parents were very liberal and both had very strong ethos in doing what you were best at and not what the normal path in school that teachers and parents often use in bringing up their children. I was given complete freedom from my parents to follow my passions.

My parents recognized this in me early on and never tried to force me into higher studies, but supported me to follow my passion and explore what drew my attention and where my greatest outlet was for creativity. I was never judged by my parents that I was an average "C" student. Instead I was supported and encouraged to follow my passion and skills, to discover what interested me in my life. Both of my parents were this way. My father was always venturing into new business careers and my mother was a working professional woman in a time where most women stayed home and raised the kids. Whereas in today's world both parents work, back in the 1950s and 60s this was not normal. My parents were great role models on how one needs to self-actualize as an individual and to not fear venturing beyond the accepted norm of one's collected conscious.

In school I avoided every science class and struggled with the mandatory course in Algebra. I had to take Algebra twice and required a tutor to help me through passing this class in mathematics. I just felt I was not a smart student. Instead I took almost every art course I could for my elective classes. This was one of those major glues that gave me focus and meaning.

The story goes that my father's family originally immigrated in the 1840s to the United States from Austria. I calculate I'm a fifth generation American. My father was abandoned by his father at six years old, during the depression of the 30s in the United States. He, his sister and mother lived in the depression ghetto of New York City called "Hell's Kitchen". From a very early age he learned to survive on the streets and managed to make money for his mother and sister. Coming from a Jewish ethnic background he was competing with other cultures in the ghetto to grab a piece of the American dream off the streets. It was a really rough place to grow up without the guidance of a father figure. It is places like this where organized crime in the United States found a foothold during the prohibition of the 20s and the depression in the 30s. He was on the streets in the middle of the Irish and Italian cultures, often clashing and fighting for a small piece of the turf. He was really a smart, clever and intelligent guy who never finished High School.

Dropping out after the 10th grade of high school he pursued every possible opportunity that came his way. He was brilliant at math and had a photographic memory. In his most successful career as a Stock Investment Manager, one could sense his quick mind in math and the photographic memory served him in the field of stock trading, pre-computers. Throughout my childhood he was a real entrepreneur. From starting out after World War II helping my uncle with wholesale produce business, to owning a furniture store, then a restaurant and finally a successful career as a Stock Investment Manager for the wealthy of Beverly Hills. All this without a High School diploma. He had a rare ability to pick himself up from the ashes and build whatever he put his head to. While growing up, my Dad would always remind me of this, hoping that he could instill in me this ability to provide for myself if he was ever to die or leave me. His form of tough love was that I learn to be able to survive and even better, thrive on my own abilities and wit. I can say with confidence he did personally impress on me and before his passing, he was able to see and be proud of what I have achieved by my own abilities.

My mother was raised by Russian Jewish immigrants fleeing persecution from the Czar of Russia at the turn of the 20th century. She was born and raised in Long Island, New York. They were middle class and my grandfather was a tailor and in the rag business of New York. He was an atheist intellectual who made sure both of his daughters were given a solid education growing up in America. My mother was very rare in that she graduated from college when very few women even went. Aside from a college degree from the University of New York, she majored in business management. A very rare and difficult path for women to enter back in those days of the 1930s. She went on to be a very successful buyer and manager for one of the USA's largest department store chains. My mother worked all the time I was growing up. During the 50s and 60s this was a rare family structure, though now it has become the norm. From both of my parents I was raised to believe if I wanted anything in life I would have to go out and earn it. Nothing was ever served to me on a silver platter. When I turned 16, I also had to demonstrate that I could earn money before my parents would chip in to help if I wanted a new surfboard or car. Learning to work at an early age has guided me through my many years as an artist and business person: skills to create and achieve with my own abilities and to be self-sufficient at an early age; the strength and skill to pick myself up, dust myself off after a failure and move forward.

To this day I am eternally grateful to both my parents for instilling in me the belief and the abilities to continue forward in life and not to fall deep into a trench of self-pity, not to get lost in failure and fall into depression. When a challenge would come my way, knock me down, appear as though there was no light at the end of the tunnel, I learned to never be defeated. I always took the challenge to turn things around and attempt to make things better. Running one's own business and especially around a luxury item I have encountered my fair share in the 30 plus years of being self-employed. Defeats can have a way of making one stronger and more resilient and in my case even more determined to succeed against all obstacles.

More often than not, when a highly successful person who is willing to be humble and honest will tell you they have failed more often than they have succeeded. And the failures would often be major losses or blunders. But from their failures they learned, adapted and changed for the positive in their life. It has proved to be a major quality in character and personality that would lead them to their ultimate success in life. They have made some of the biggest mistakes but it just did not stop them. My father was this way, he succeeded and failed many times while I was growing up. I can reflect on my life now, how numerous times it appeared that my business as a Gem Artist was about to go under. I can reflect now how I would not stay stuck for too long in depression but eventually pick myself up, dust myself off and re-invent my career. I learned with every failure to pick myself up and start anew. I have basically worked for myself and earned a living since I was 15 years old.

I believe it was the very successful impressionist artist, Monet who said, "I have never met a real 'living" successful artist in his/her life without being a very successful business person as well." I could not agree more with him.

4

ON A JOURNEY OF DISCOVERY OUTSIDE THE BOX

· Standing on the Precipice as a Fool

"East, west, south or north makes little difference. No matter what your destination, just be sure to make every journey a journey within. If you travel within, you'll travel the whole wide world and beyond."
The Forty Rules of Love by **Elif Shafak**

An Adventure of Wonder and Fear: Wandering in the Art of Europe, the Ruins of Italy and Greece, and Following Ancient Spice Trails to Cultures of the Middle East and the Mystical Realms of Central Asia

I can still see, to this day, the look on my mother's face as she was dropping me off on the I-10 freeway on-ramp in West Los Angeles, 43 years ago. This wide-eyed, scared look that she may never see her son again. The fear was in her eyes, but true to my mother today, she never stopped me from making my own life choices regardless of her own feelings and personal fear. She has always been good at keeping them to herself.

I consider this one of my mother's greatest virtues. Not letting her fears get in the way of her children's ability to seek and find their own creativity and personal genius in life. Fortunately, my very liberal parents supported me in whatever I chose to do with my life. They supported this decision of dropping out of college and travel. Their basic answer to this was, "It's your life and you must follow what gives you passion." Both my mother and father supported this belief and gave us kids freedom to choose how and what to do with our lives. I know that travel to faraway lands like Iran, Turkey, Afghanistan and India scared my mother but she would never have shared this with me at the time. It was not until many years later in her life that I would learn the truth of her true feelings. Both of my parents supported and believed in me being my own person. My mother is living proof to this day in her life aged over 100 years old and still functioning clearly in her mind, to be open and willing to change and grow. I think I learned from her to never stop learning and changing in one's life. To this day I believe one is never too old to learn something new and be willing to change no matter how old one is. This is so true in gemology and gem cutting in that there is a never-ending learning curve about the subject. There is always a new gem material being discovered somewhere in the world, a new mine source, some new enhancement and for sure, new ways to carve and cut gemstone. Forty years into my career I feel like my very best work is still ahead of me.

Recently, I was visiting my mother in Los Angeles. During

my visit, my two brothers and I had dinner together. During the conversation, all three of us, my older brother Wayne, my younger brother Harvey and I all shared similar stories confirming this same experience while growing up. We were given way more freedom at a very early age to venture out into the world without parental oversight, at ages like 13 and 14, where we would hitchhike through the state of California, backpack in the High Sierra wilderness country or pile in a car and go on a surf safari down the coast of California. Risky adventures for adults, let alone young teenagers like myself and my brothers. Looking back on these formative years, I can now see they were preparation for when I stepped out of my mom's car on that fated on-ramp 43 years ago, placed my thumb out, and began the journey that took me to faraway places and around the world during what would be my real college education.

In the year 1973, one and half years into College and two years into these multiple strange mystical experiences, I was without a compass. I was struggling to find my way through life. I felt exposed, vulnerable and had only my wits and judgment to blindly find my way, because there seemed to be no true mentor to help me find a way forward. There were road signs and clues but I had not found anyone or any written doctrine that gave me a sense of safety and security. I was struggling to see how to make these two apparent paradoxical worlds integrate into some form of "normal" balance with me. I was feeling lost and out of place in my own culture. Beyond this I had no real clue who or what to turn to for some road signs forward in life. The life I knew no longer made real sense. All I knew up to this point was what my parents, teachers and culture said what life is all about. I was now wildly trying to understand and function this totally new dimension in my life within. It had turned my understanding of what life is supposed to be turned upside down and inside out. It felt like it was time to explore outside my culture's box of beliefs and attitudes.

What motivated me to drop out of college age 20 was when I began to have spontaneous out-of-body states of awareness and mystical experiences. They led me to the very core of an atom and to the far reaches of this planet in search of the indescribable yet sublime world and to the very nature of life and reality itself. From these initial mystical and spiritual experiences, my life going forward was completely focused on this sublime inner world and dimensions. I have devoted my life to expressing these experiences through art and beauty as the best way to communicate these deeper recesses of our own consciousness and life as we know it, hidden in these micro and macro worlds of the universe. It was these very mystical experiences, along with being bored in college, that led me to drop out of school and travel the world. I wanted to search for answers in different lands and cultures beyond my West Coast American upbringing. I was longing to break out of my box and peek beyond what I knew up to this point to be true. Pushing the very boundaries of my own "beliefs and attitudes".

I longed for something outside my Western upbringing. In my first year of college I had studied comparative religions and opened my mind to ancient philosophies and religions such as Hinduism, Buddhism, Tao, Judea-Christianity as well as Islam. I was in search of meaning and wanted to understand the strange, mystical experiences that were happening spontaneously in my life at the time. I could begin to glean that below every major religion in the world today was a spiritual essence that the universe held mysteries that the physical eyes were blind to. In college I studied with a Sufi master who started to help me to see the world not through my physical eyes but though mystical inner awareness. I began to open a more real world than what I was living and growing up in Los Angeles, the world of glamour and outside image.

So, I chose to leave my life as I had known it and travel the world for answers. This was my new international college where I hoped to find answers to my confusion. Looking back now, I can clearly see it was a time in my life where I truly was able to live my live with complete "Freedom without any responsibilities" (Lazaris). I had no wife, children or job at that time that kept me bound to my life in America. I could choose to go anywhere and do anything that moved me. I would say over and over again in my travels during this time, "I am like a leaf in the wind and each day I wake up to see where the wind blows me." It was a very treasured time in my life. I was changed forever by it, in oh so many ways.

Once I hit the road and pushed beyond my safe and somewhat idyllic life in California little did I realize what was really in store for me. Little did I know I was going to be pushed to the very primal instinct to survive. I was not just transformed by the exposure to foreign and exotic cultures but by the very primal fear that I had to face several times on my travels. The sheer raw vulnerability of being in a very foreign, often a very geographically remote culture, in dangerous life/death situations. Fear was pressing right up against a very natural instinct to survive.

You may wonder what this has to do with my art and gem cutting. It has a lot to do with it. People often ask when I'm working on a very rare piece, in the hundreds of thousands of dollars range, " Aren't you scared when you're working on the stone of such high value?". My answer is simple today, "No, I am very calm and focused. It's like a Zen meditation for me. I only work on the stone when I am clear and ready. Plus, I don't think about the value, I'm only focused on doing the right thing with this gem". I believe my early travels exposed me to so much of what fear can be that now, in my wisdom years I do fear, but I see clearly how to handle it and move forward. I don't get paralyzed by fear. Fear is a good thing in it that it is meant to be an internal early warning system to survive. This is in our very DNA. Sometimes it's an exterior fear, like a train barreling down on me. Other times it is an emotional fear.

From my travels to remote foreign cultures to cutting that million dollar gemstone, I know with a greater sense of grace, "Show up, pay attention and do the right thing." Fear to me now is what is was naturally meant to be, an early warning sign things are not quite right. I can be in danger, so I need to slow down, take a close look and then choose how to respond. Gem cutting is exactly like that. It requires an absolute clarity of mind. I show up, fully present and aware of its rarity and value. I take a very, very close look, often to the dismay of the collector or dealer who owns the stone that it's taking so long to fill that order. I have been known to study the stone for over a year, or even three, before I will lay the first cut. With patience and clarity, each time that gem touches that Diamond grinding wheel I am of one mind, aware of exactly how much to remove. I feel like I am in a state of grace performing with complete elegance and beauty. I am letting this very rare gemstone, that has been lying dormant for at least 40 to 50 million years, talk to me and guide me to its next state which is about to be traumatically transformed by my hands and being. This is a very powerful mantra I repeat daily every time I touch a gemstone, big or small. It has nothing to do with human placed value upon it, but with Nature's own wonder of rarity that every gemstone has value, regardless of the monetary amount arbitrarily placed on it by commerce.

To return to my life-changing journey that brought about this understanding and command of fear, my journey begins around the world at the age of 20. I hitchhiked from Los Angeles across the southern states of the US to land in Florida at its most southern tip, Key West. This was mostly uneventful except for the few crazy people who picked me up in their car as I hitchhiked through the south of the US. Though I found myself in a few compromising situations traveling across the US, it was nothing compared to what was about to happen to me. I flew from Miami, to the Bahamas and then onward to Luxembourg and the European continent. Within 48 hours of landing on the European continent, I was about to get tested in the most frightful experience I had ever encountered: a wild car ride and an unforgettable evening that left an indelible mark on my life forever. This first 48 hours occurred in a foreign land where I did not speak the language nor have a clue where I was.

Meeting a French Comrade in Arms and the Hole in the Fence

Twenty four hours after landing in Luxembourg and during my first night in a European Youth Hostel, I placed my thumb out in the direction of Italy. I'm headed to see the masters of the renaissance art world whom I admired and studied in school. It's a very cold, cloudy, wet and snowy day so I was extremely happy when anyone would pick me up and move me down the road closer to my destination to the South.

Shortly into the day I'm picked up by two French students on their way back to school. One speaks enough English that I can understand about every third word. I have absolutely no sense of the French language so I'm in the dark about most of what's being said in the car.

A short distance in our journey down the road they pick up a second hitchhiker. He is also French and is headed in about the same direction as I am. The two students in the car sort of translate to me that this second hitchhiker is basically headed in my same direction and I should travel along with him once they drop us off down the highway. Sounds reasonable to me. They also vaguely translate that he is headed to see some of his old friends and has invited me to tag along with him where I can have a bed to sleep and a warm meal for the night before I head further on my journey. Sounds even more inviting and like a fun adventure to meet the locals on my second day in a foreign land. Little did I know at the time that the two students seemed to have left out the details as to where this second hitchhiker was actually headed and who he was. This is where the bend in the road becomes one of the most frightful experiences in my life.

As we disembark from the car and the two students wish us well on our journey this second hitchhiker who appears to be a very nice guy begins to say in broken English, "Comrades, comrades, going to see comrades", and at the same time he holds up his arms and crosses them at his wrist. All I could understand was comrade. Surely he must have meant his friends, but the crossing of his wrist made no sense to me at the time. I would learn much later in the evening the true meaning of the crossed wrist.

We get picked up and it seems the next driver did not speak English either, but I could sense he was going exactly where my new friend and fellow hitchhiker wanted us to be going. I was delighted and a bit relieved, until the car leaves the main highway that is leading me to my ultimate destination and makes a turn down some small country road. I begin to get nervous, completely lost now and at the mercy of my fellow traveler I am now clueless to where we are and where we're really going. I never felt threatened by my fellow hitchhiker, but I did feel completely powerless and at the mercy of someone I did not know and could not even converse with. As soon as I made my fear known to him, even though I'm sure he did not understand what I was saying, he seemed to sense my panic and just kept repeating, "Comrades, Comrades", smiled and gave that universal hand gesture of putting food in one's mouth. Communicating in that universal language of hand gestures, which we both understood, reminded me that there was food waiting for us at the end of this journey. I was powerless, lost as to where we were going and now it was the middle of the night with not a star or moon to light my way. It was pitch black out and it seemed to compound how I felt emotionally, complete lost and in a panic fear state. By this time there was nothing for me to do but continue down this road and see where he was taking me. Remember I'm now only 48 hours into my journey away from the only home or country I'd ever known.

It's now the middle of the night and the car just stops at the crest and bend in this narrow country road in the middle of nowhere, in the pitch blackness. As we get out of the car I look up and there is a huge locked gate and above is a sign that references the French Military Army. Here we are in the middle of the night, in the middle of what seems like nowhere and I'm standing in front of a French Military Army base. So this is what my co-hitchhiker kept saying when he repeated comrade. The pieces start to come together in my brain. His friends are in the army and he has come here to visit them. I instantly freak out. I tell him in English, "I can't go on this army base, are you crazy?" This did nothing for my case since I know he understood absolutely nothing. But my knee jerk response was to speak it out as though I needed him to understand what I was going though at this very moment. I'm sure he understood absolutely nothing I was saying. He just keeps gesturing me to follow him. Here I am in the middle of nowhere in the middle of the night, clueless where I am geographically, with a total stranger, standing in front of a French Army base. My mind is racing. What am I going to do now?

He appears to me to be very excited and to be there to see old friends, clearly ignoring my panic for sure. He instructs me to follow him as we walk around the base's outer wall with a high chain link fence that encloses this army base. I feel helpless and at this point my only choice seems to be to follow him and trust him with my life. We come to the back of the base where there is a hole cut into this chain link fence. He instructs me to crawl through this break in the fence. I remember standing there panicking, unable to move. Going forward seemed uncertain peril, going back meant I was completely lost, in the middle of nowhere in the dead of night. Do I go through the fence, as a foreigner on a military army base? Looking back now it was an absolutely insane choice.

It seemed like eternity as I stood there trying to weigh my options with my brain in overdrive in total panic and rare fear.

He jumps through the hole standing on the other side waving me to come in. What to do? I'm not sure what came over me but I remember almost in a hypnotic state stepping through this hole into a completely foreign and dangerous space. A foreigner, entering a foreign country's army base. It was only my first few days since departing America, and it seems it was not going well for me. We walk up to a building in the back of the base and my fellow traveler starts to rapidly knock on this nondescript door. As the door opens there are two fellows dressed in full army fatigues. They appear so overjoyed in this moment to see their friend, I was literally invisible to their eyes for what seemed an eternity to me. Here's this l'Américain hippie with long hair and a beard standing there on their army base. They have us enter this building that turns out to be the mess hall of this military base.

So here I am: the meal he promised is the army mess hall and the place to sleep for the night is a French Army base. This is definitely not a good situation to find myself in.

Neither of his friends speak English, so I'm even more lost as to what to do or to figure out where I am. As he and his friends are talking with exhilaration between one another I am in complete fear and panic knowing full well I should not be where I am. I remember pulling out my road map of Europe with major highways designated on it, trying frantically to find out where I am. The three of them are enjoying the company and seem oblivious to my state of dread. At one point, they turn to the map and start almost mind tripping to different places on the map that either they have been or wish to go. Clueless as I'm frantically pointing on the map and screaming, "Where are we? Where am I here on this map at this very moment?" I never did find out. Oh yeah, and the meal: a couple cans of Spam and a French loaf bread. Dinner!

About half an hour into this strange, surreal situation a very loud knock came from the front door to the mess hall. The two soldiers, get up, go to the door and open maybe only six inches (12 cm) or so, enough to peak out and for whoever outside to openly peak in. I could make out from the distance there were at least eight uniformed soldiers standing at the door. A strong and what appeared to me to be an intense and vigorous dialogue was going back and forth like a ping pong match between the mess hall soldiers and those standing outside. It was for sure way past midnight by now. Not a normal time for soldiers to be up unless they're on duty. Oh, my God - my fear at this point was rocketing through the roof. What seemed like at least a couple minutes to me, the two mess hall soldiers finally let in who was standing outside. Nine come filing in, in uniform, turn and all look at me. One of the mess hall soldiers says, "L'Américain" followed by many French words. Following this, all at once, the whole crew who just filed through the door come running over to shake my hand. Surreal! The real purpose of this midnight raid was not to catch a foreigner on base but to raid the kitchen for a late-night supper, all undercover. I could not believe what was happening right in front of my eyes. I was about to sit down and have a gourmet French dinner of steak, potatoes and red wine. This was right out of some foreign film scene I remember going to see as a boy. Paradoxes of something that should be straight and in control turns out to be a scene with all the actors in full character and very animated in expression.

The night turns from sheer dread to absolute fun and my first exhilarating cultural exchange with people from another land and of a different language. Luckily for me, one of the nine I'm now dining with speaks decent English so now we can converse. They all have questions about what is America really like, especially Hollywood and California surfing. Remember the year is 1973 and global travel is not what it is today. I soon learn the real story of my hitchhiking buddy who brought me to this army base. Turns out he was in the army here with all his buddies but was dishonorably discharged, I do not know for what. He was even thrown in jail for a spell of time. I now knew what he meant with his raised arms crossed at the wrist. This was the universal symbol for being shackled in handcuffs. God, I don't know if I would have been there that night had I known the true story from the start of my travels with him.

So, the night up to now turns out to be quite a wild and scary ride that ends with this huge emotional release and unexpected fun story that I know I'll never forget for the rest of my life. But the night does not end there. As we wrap up dinner and all the dishes are washed and the kitchen cleaned like nothing happened in the mess hall, the English-speaking solider comes up and tells me where I'm to sleep tonight.

He starts out by saying his buddies will walk me and my hitchhiking, newly discovered ex-con friend across the base grounds to one of the barracks where there are two beds to sleep. Then he says, "Don't get caught on the base, because if you're discovered they will most likely throw you in the brig for being a foreign spy on military property". Great, just when I thought I was out of the dark woods, this one sentence sent me back in absolute fear again. Then, to throw more salt on my emotional vulnerability he then said, "And be sure to get up before the bugle horn goes off in the morning and leave, then you'll be alright." I can tell you I was not all right for the rest of the night. I'm sure I did not sleep more than half an hour. I was in so much fear now of being discovered and thrown in jail.

So, as we cross the base's grounds, a patrolling guard approaches us. I can remember seeing three strips on his sleeve, possibly the equivalent to a sergeant in our army, stopping us in our dash across the base at an ungodly hour for any army personnel to be moving. I am thinking "Oh my God this is it, I'm busted" as his flashlight is glaring in my eyes, and I try to adjust to the light to see his face. There was what seemed an intense interchange with my hitchhiking buddy, the solider walking us and this patrolling guard. This lasts for about 30 seconds until he just waves us on and points to the barracks we were headed to. I'm thinking what kind of Army is this? I'm an American, full on hippie with a backpack on a foreign military base and no one seems to care. They seem more intrigued by me being a novel American in their midst rather than worried I'm some sort of spy.

We get to the barracks where there must be at least 20 sleeping soldiers in their beds lined up going down both side of the walls. Just as we enter there is one empty bed and I'm instructed to sleep here. My hitchhiking friend and fellow soldier seem to almost disappear in the dark as they walk down this long narrow building. Now I have no idea where my hitchhiking buddy is sleeping. I curl up in this bed but don't seem to get any sleep the whole night, worried if I don't get off this army base before the bugle goes off in the morning I'm busted.

Sometime late in the night or early in the morning - since I have absolutely no sense of what time it is - I'm so worried the bugle is about to go off, that I get up to walk down this long narrow building with bodies asleep on both sides to where I think my buddy is sleeping. I walk up and gently shake the covers so as not to disturb any of the others sleeping. This guy turns around, and he's not my hitchhiking buddy for sure - cursing me in French. Luckily I didn't understand what he said but it was clear he was not happy and wondering who the hell this guy is. Sheepishly, I walk back to my bunk more freaked and nervous, feeling very alone and uncertain. By this time in the night I have faced the teeth of fear several times, with this crazy rollercoaster emotional experience wrapped in just a few hours.

Sometime in the morning I finally feel this shake and my new friend is waking me and instructing it's time to go. By this point I'm so ready to get off this base and on my way. This night has been one of the most difficult and emotionally edgy moments I think I had ever experienced up to this point in my life. We walk across the still dark night sky on this base tracing our steps back to the mess hall.

There in the hall are his two army buddies who first greeted us the night before, standing over a huge soup pot of café au lait. I'm being handed a huge 20oz bowl filled with coffee that was brewed in milk and a loaf of sourdough bread. Breakfast French Army style. As I'm enjoying my morning wake up meal the bugle goes off and I quickly glance over to my guide who brought me here and now I'm waiting to leave with him. He gives me a look not to worry and just hang tight where we are. The hall begins to fill quite quickly with the full staff of soldiers from the base. They all walk in, look my way and seem absolutely unconcerned by this out of place presence on a military base. I'm in this dream state, almost this after-glow euphoric place, following a night consumed of mostly terror and dread state of being.

Then, almost without a single clue and no rhyme or reason, my ex-con hitchhiking buddy comes walking over to me and signals it's time to go. He leads me out the back door of the mess hall and to the hole in the fence. Excited to leave, I'm the first one jumping through. I turn to him, expecting him to follow, but he is standing on the other side motioning to me he is staying and is saying goodbye here. Completely relieved to be out of this place and no longing fearing something that could fall my way I turn and walk the way we entered the night before. I get to the road and just start walking the way the car came that dropped us off in the dark of night. Though I still had no clue where I was on the map I knew that if I walked the way I came I would get back to the main highway.

As memory has it, it was somewhere between three to five miles when I hit the main road that would set my course back to Switzerland and Italy, my first intended goal on my travels in Europe. The humor at the end of this story is, within five minutes of me standing on the main highway hitchhiking, a police car with two officers stop and begin to interrogate me. I'm still in this very ecstatic state of relief from the night of shear fear and extreme vulnerability. Inside I'm laughing that after all this, when I'm no longer in harm's way, I'm being frisked, having to show my passport, explain my travels and have my backpack searched for drugs.

I'm laughing inside knowing these police have nothing on me and the comedy of events unfolding that I came through all of this with no harm. Looking back, I actually had an experience I will remember and cherish for years to come.

It was one of several on my journeys of world travels where I would be in harm's way, facing my worst fears, maintaining my outer composure and coming through unharmed; in many cases triumphing in those intense moments. It is where now I can look back and see I was being tested to the extremes of how fear can either heighten one's ability to focus on the moment and the details or completely paralyze the mind and have things possibly go drastically wrong. Looking back now on experiences like this one, my ability to work with very rare and extremely expensive gemstones I know the zone where I'm feeling in a still state of mind, focused on the here and now, aware of so many of the subtleties, such as the sound of the stone on the grinding wheel, the feel of the stone as it's been ground away. My first real direct experience of handling fear without losing my mind.

Once back on track and the road to discovery, my main goal of my travels was to see the masters of fine art whom I had admired and studied during the Renaissance period in history. I spent six months traveling through Italy, taking in the long history from Roman times to the art of the master that left a legacy of art in the Vatican. I even traveled to the tiny island of Elba, where Napoleon was placed in exile after almost conquering all of Europe. I found myself, a kid from Los Angeles, growing up around movie stars and the illusion of the silver screen, walking in the footsteps of history. On the very paths that Michelangelo walked in Italy, and Napoleon walked at the end of his life on the Isle of Elba, I walked too. I got to stand in front of the David in Florence and feel the blood flowing through his veins. I was mesmerized by all the art and particularly the "The Birth of Venus" from one of my favorite Renaissance masters, Botticelli (1445-1510).

From Italy, I ferried across the Aegean Sea to the island of Corfu and then to Greece to take in the birth of the Western world and stand among ancient ruins that have been sitting on this Earth for over 4000 years. I walked the ancient goat paths, through centuries old olive groves to feel the mystical history of the Oracle of Delphi. It was in Delphi that I experienced a tremendous déjà vu mystical experience that I had been there before, standing before the ancient fountains where the virgin oracles would reveal the mysteries and prophecies of life. I began to feel that the world held such wonders and mysteries that I had never experienced before. Moments like this I have come to realize there is no past, present or future but timeless realms of pure consciousness. I can look back now and see how these experiences helped formulate my life as an artist. It was here that I began to experience life way beyond a kid growing up in Los Angeles, where history only dated back no more than two centuries. The world holds many wonders that cannot be explained in simple language. I had stirred and awoke by traveling outside my box, an ancient mystical part of my soul and touched the Earth in a way my childhood and school could never have ignited me.

After six months of traveling through Italy and Greece I reached a point of wondering what next and where to go from here. Now fully saturated with the art of Europe and the ancient ruins of Greece I was still longing for answers. I was still seeking answers for this mystical realm that was stirred inside my soul but still did not know where to seek them.

On a whim I decided to fly to Istanbul. This proved to be an adventure and journey that took me into a world of mystery and magic that from a Western standpoint I had never encountered. It was also the beginning of understanding those mystical experience that were spontaneously occurring within me. It was in Istanbul where one can feel the unique blend of Occidental and Oriental beliefs, co-mingling and cross fertilizing for centuries. The crossroads between what I felt were two very different understandings of our world. For most of my youth and adolescence I felt somewhat of a loner and out of place in my own culture. I can describe it as being a boundary dweller where I had one foot in two very different, opposite worlds but could not understand why. It was not until I entered the world of the Orient did I began to feel this void that had commenced as a child could finally be answered. It was here, in Istanbul, where I got my first internal sense that answers to my perplexing questions of these mystical realms could be answered. I now felt I was on the trail that could possibly give me insight to my inner world of mystery and magic.

My childhood was completely devoid of any knowledge or upbringing of Western religions. Though I am of Jewish decent, my family only participated in the religious holidays as a cultural social interaction. I was raised an atheist. I had very little knowledge and had not read the Old or New Testament until I was in my 20s, when I began to search for answers for these occurring mystical experiences I was having. I had no idea what was happening to me so I turned to world religions for the possible answers to this strange and mystical realm on the inner. Dissatisfied by Western religion's ability to explain what was happening to me, I turned to Eastern religions where spirituality and mysticism have a deep and ancient root that goes back for centuries long before the birth of Christianity.

Still unable to find answers and dissatisfied, I then turned to world travel as a way to see how the rest of the world lived outside of my Judeo-Christian Western upbringing. For the first time since leaving my life behind in California, I began to feel I was on the scent of answers my soul was so desperately seeking once I crossed this invisible border between Greece and Turkey. It was in Turkey where I could see how different others in the world could live and see the world. It was here that I could visually see that one's logic and understanding of the world is shaped by one's culture and upbringing. Mine was one of materialism and personal achievement, this Near East and Far East was shaped by century old beliefs of an inner mystical and spiritual world, focused around devotion and view of a very different perspective God.

A Wild Ride on the Orient Express: Heading East Facing the Dark Side of Life in a Foreign Land

As my journey continued heading East, now to India, I boarded the train in Istanbul for Tehran, Iran. The Orient Express train would head overland through the mountains of Turkey and cross the border into Iran. As I boarded the train I met up with a few other Westerners heading East and also met and connected with a French woman. During this scheduled five-day train ride there were two very dangerous and possibly explosive encounters that could have gone terribly wrong.

The first experience was as we boarded this crowded train and while we're walking the aisles, these young Turkish men kept groping, touching and pinching the rears of the Western women on the train. For some reason, they thought this was acceptable to do with Western women, thinking women from the West are 'loose' so they could acceptably get away with this. Whereas in their Muslim culture, it is completely forbidden and totally unacceptable for them to do it with their women. After several encounters, I had finally had it - especially after they did this to my French girlfriend. I stood up and commanded that they stop this action.

The next thing I realize is one man who pinched the rear of my girlfriend, pulls out a knife and is now threatening me. All of a sudden I realize I'm in a life or death situation and outnumbered by his friends who for sure all are carrying knives. What to do? Immediately a crowd forms. His friends all crowd me and all the Westerners who are on the train gather in support of my precarious situation, and are now forming what we say here in America a "Mexican standoff", like one would see in a Western shoot out. Though I'm sure it's just for a few seconds, it now feels like I spent an eternity standing there. The air feels tense, thick, and emotions are heightened.

Here I am in a foreign culture, in a very unbalanced situation. This is where all my composure and sensitivity comes in to play. Uncertain as to what to do, my reflex is to calm the heightened nerves of all who are standing off against one another. My first response is to raise my hands and lower them in a calming gesture, smile and say, "easy, easy". The one holding the knife, along with his half dozen Turkish young men, and the 12 or so Western traveling men facing down one another as everything could go very wrong in an instant.

I'm not quite sure what calmed the air: my gesture of raising my hands with palms down and lowering my hands motioning to stay calm, or just that this man with a knife was not really serious. I have no idea since we could not communicate by words. All I remember is a smile comes across this young Turkish man's face, we all start to laugh and the situation returns to some form of normal. We all begin to laugh and joke, the moment passes without an incidence erupting into deadly violence.

The other situation is, as we continued on the Orient Express heading overland to Tehran, we encounter a major snow storm that locked the train down in five-foot snow drifts. We are now waiting for a steam locomotive to push us out since the locomotive pulling us is not strong enough to get us through these snow drifts. For two days we were stuck in the snow and everyone was feeling a bit of cabin fever. I decide to step off the train and walk out about 100 yards. I bend down, place my hands in the snow, close my eyes and slip into a meditative state. The next thing I hear is a voice shouting form the train in English, "Glenn, look out!" Without moving I open my eyes as I peer through my legs looking back at the train. I see this young Turkish man run up behind me thinking he will surprise me by pushing me over in the snow. I'm guessing he and his friend will get a good laugh on my account.

So I lay dormant, not moving, bent over remaining still and calm, I wait for that exact moment to move. Like a scene is some Kung Fu movie, as he is right behind me I raise up, grab him around the neck and flip him over my body throwing him five feet in front of me. Here I am, only 5"3", small in stature, he - being at least a head taller than me - goes whizzing in the air. So instead of me being the brunt of the joke, all of a sudden he is the one being laughed at. Well, you can imagine his anger and frustration. The next thing I realize, out come all his friends, a dozen or so, circling me like Indians around a wagon train of the Wild West. I appear to be completely outnumbered. They then begin to throw snowballs at me. This is their revenge. At this moment it appears like a harmless snow fight. But I'm completely uncertain the knives at any moment could come back out towards me. Luckily, my Western friends are watching this and quickly come to my aid. Snowballs are flying everywhere. In the mayhem I slip out of the line of fire and sights of these young Turks and disappear back on to the train. Apparently once they realized I'm gone the fight ends and all goes calm again.

As I reflect back upon these experiences I can't help but think how my calm composure and quick reflexes might have been the ingredient to deflecting situations that could have gone terribly wrong, especially when two very different cultures and mind sets are in a moment of heightened tension and possible violence. Though I'm not sure what really lessened the tension in both occurrences, I know now that I found this inner calm and clear state of mind in the midst of chaos. I know that I am constantly being bombarded by various approaches to life as I travel to remote regions of the world, where I must remain open and tolerant to how there is just so many different ways to see one's world and how various people of different countries react to the same situation.

I know this to be true today as I work alongside my Indian team of gem cutters in the factory at Pink City, India owned by my good friend and partner Manuj Goyal. When I first started to teach my cutters to learn new techniques in carving the TorusRing, it was not perfect by a long shot. Instead of judging and critiquing how wrong their work was, I would complement them on their progress, gently point out what they could do better on the next attempt. Having lived in India as a young man for two years I have grown to understand the Indian culture and how very different it is to my American upbringing. What I've discovered was that each attempt, by my encouraging them to improve the cut, the end result kept getting better and more refined. They would work harder to improve on their own, wanting to please me more at each attempt at cutting the TorusRing cut. I think this is true for all cultures and people. In the West, and I know especially in my younger days, I would be quick to judge and point out what is wrong straight out of the gate.

I know for myself, we tend to quickly judge and lack tolerance in the world today, each of us thinking we're better than others and our way is the right way. I've come to realize there is no right way. My friend Manuj has reflected back to me that he was impressed how I would show tolerance with their work and accept the cut as good enough to move the whole project forward. Allowing each collection we were working on for Gemporia to be good enough in a step-by-step process. It was not about perfection from the start for me. I've learned to let each step be good enough, each new collection building on the last. Making significant progress with each new collection. Today, after four and half years, the work is really good and their love to achieve their best motivates them to achieve excellence. The product is now miles ahead and far better than when we first started. I can see in each and every one of them there is this drive to constantly stretch what is possible out of their respect and love for me. There is a fine line between being judgmental and having good judgment.

In moments of danger or chaos one must stay calm and focus on the prize. Fear can be a warning to the impeding danger or it can devastate one's judgment in the face of fire. Having moments like this, on this train in a very foreign land could have gone very wrong. But instead I found myself staying calm and focused, doing everything I could to defuse a very precarious situation. This may seem like a completely unrelated experience to my art and gem cutting, but in so many ways it has served me, as it has stayed with me all this time. I know fear. I have learned to allow it to be my friend, to serve me in my many travels to remote places and divergent cultures, personally facing a life-threatening disease in my life, and yes when I am sitting at the wheel working on a million-dollar gemstone, I know how to be in that zone of calm and clarity. Not to move until my inner voice gives me that go ahead.

This was still the time before the Iranian Revolution. There was little fear with regard to being a target because I was an American. The year was 1973 and Americans in this part of the world were still welcomed with open arms. We were looked up to as the shining country everyone else in the world admired and wanted to strive to be like with all our material successes. Everywhere I went in Turkey, Iran and Afghanistan I was greeted with open arms, invited into homes and asked constantly to sit and share tea or a meal. Whether it was some canvas tent in the middle of the barren land of Afghanistan, a dug wash mud floor hut of Agra or the home of a police chief in the Jungles of Southern India, I was treated as a special guest and was honored like some major dignitary. To these people in these remote places it was considered a great honor and big deal to sit and share tea or a meal, and for me to tell stories about what life is like in America. It was an incredible experience to exchange and learn about their culture as much as they wanted to hear about my country and culture. Life in these parts of the world were still untouched by wars, terrorism and the materialism of the West. I was getting out more about their lives and culture than they were getting from me about my life growing up in America. I was traveling in foreign exotic lands that were still the same as they had been for centuries: rural, rugged and primitive by Western standards at that time. I was getting what my soul had been seeking the moment I set out on my journey many months ago. I had begun to find the fulfillment my heart was craving, as I wandered this exotic mystical land and the fabled spice trails of the East. Life at this time in these remote places was the same as it had been for centuries. I was living my dream the day I set out to discover what my soul and spirit were trying to get me to see in these mystical experiences I was having.

I can look back now and see how significant this journey has been in my life and how it has formed and molded my life's work. Opening to a remote, very foreign culture has had a profound impact in my life, art and spiritual philosophy. I've learned what the true meaning of tolerance is, when one steps outside their safe confines and defined culture. To be exposed to a completely different sensibility and logic to living one's life, I have come to realize there is no one way to live one's life. These experiences have had an indelible impact on my life forever. I was now living the University of Life way beyond anything I could have imagined before leaving America and choosing to drop out of college. And it has continued to serve me in so many ways now that travel to very remote and exotic places in search of gemstone material for my art.

Buckminster Fuller used to use the analogy of the trim tab on a large cargo ocean vessel to how change can occur in one's life. The trim tab is a very small rudder on this huge, multi-football field size cargo ship. In order to make a 90 degree turn the captain would set the rudder by only one small degree. Eventually this immense cargo ship would be travelling in a completely different direction. Ships of this size just can't turn like you think of how you turn the wheel of your car. One small change, that one degree of change in one's perception can have a huge impact on one's life and attitude. Those years were formative in my ability to feel open and at home in so many different cultures. It is so well said in Eric Weiner's book, The Geography of Genius, "On an individual level, psychologists have identified this openness to experience as the single most important trait of exceptional creative people", and in a given society "...for all cultures; every leap forward is preceded by an exposure to foreign ideas." (Page 55.) We can see in today's world where isolationism and xénophobia is forcing countries to consider closing their boundaries and the cry to remove foreigners from their lands. This is a very dangerous move and has only led to the collapse of cultures. History has shown it can only lead to wars and not progress of the human genius that I believe exists in each and every one of us. I believe what our world needs so desperately now is tolerance and not exclusivity.

My mother at the time of writing is 101 years old. An amazing feat for this day and age. When I was speaking with her physical therapist of Gerontology after she recovered from a stroke at 92, I asked him, "What do you think has been the success of my mother's amazing recovery, where many at her age would have given up and died?" His answer was to tell me about this study where they gave a series of over 200 questions to a large group of centenarians. There was only one answer that these individuals over 100 years old had in common. It was not what they ate, drank, smoked or how they lived their life. What they all had in common is that they were open and able to accept change – be it good or adverse in their life. To me this has been a driving force and what my parents passed on to me: be open, be tolerant and be willing to change and be exposed to new ideas. I have taken this advice in my life and have incorporated it into my exploration and originality to my art. In my world travels I am always exploring the ways of various and diverse cultures. I feel my art is a fusion of this philosophy.

Trapped in No Man's Land Between Afghanistan and Pakistan in the Fabled Khyber Pass

For those born before the 1990s, there was no internet, no mobile phones and no faxes. To book a phone call over land and then on the trans-Atlantic cable back home was a major effort, it was a four hour ride to the nearest town with a public phone, and often in remote places not very successful. In 1973 there was none of the new technology of the information age available.

In my early travels, over land in countries like Turkey, Iran, Afghanistan and Pakistan, one must be open and ready for the unexpected. Gemstones seem to more often than not be found in the most remote and underdeveloped places on the planet. You are totally out there with nothing more than your own good sense and mercy of the locals. I was living on the edge of reality by the age of 20. This to me is what I've referred to as 'standing on the precipice as a fool'.

This is one of those stories to this day that has left an indelible image in my mind and has proven to be one of those character-building experiences in life. I had been living in Afghanistan for just under two months and my visa was running out. I could no longer get it renewed so I was forced to leave. I did not want to return to Iran so I decided I wanted to go to India. The problem was that to get to India I had to get through Pakistan during what was then called the Islamic Conference. It was being held at the time in Pakistan. All the Islamic nations would be gathering in one of its hosting countries. It was just after the Munich Massacre, so the Islamic countries were afraid of some form of reprisal. So, Pakistan decided that it would close its border to any foreigners entering for 30 days. In order for me to get to India I had to travel through Pakistan right about this time. I was given a transit visa to enter Pakistan on or before a certain day in order to pass through Pakistan to get to India. With a handful of other Westerners, we all got on this bus in Kabul to get us to the Pakistan border before it closed in two days. It appeared to not be an issue since one could travel from Kabul to the Khyber Pass, the border, in less than one day.

Half way there of course the bus breaks down. So we frantically look for options to get us to the border before it closes. And for me it was also an issue of my visa expiring within a couple days as well. After being stuck in the hills above Kabul with a broken down bus we were able to flag a lorry that would drive us to the border. Now it was a race to get there before 5 o'clock that day in order to enter into Pakistan before our transit visa was no longer valid.

We arrived at the border literally at 5:15pm that day. Realizing we are 15 minutes late we plead with the Afghani border police to let us through. They tell us that if the Pakistani border is willing to let you through tonight we will let you exit Afghanistan tonight. They tell us they will phone the border patrol on the Pakistan side to see if they will let us in tonight. About 10 minutes later they come out of their offices and tell us that the Pakistan side said that they will let us through tomorrow morning with our visas, even though the visa was good only until today. We all felt relieved, and enjoyed our night on the Afghanistan border feeling confident we would be able to transit into and through Pakistan the next morning.

Awakening early the next morning we get our passports stamped as we exit Afghanistan and walk a quarter of a mile of what is called no man's land. This no man's land is neither Afghanistan nor Pakistan, but literally no man's country with barbed wire on both sides and guns pointed at each other. When we reach the Pakistan side we present our passports. The first thing we hear is, "Your visas are invalid. They expired yesterday." We're shocked. We tell them that the Afghanistan Border Patrol said they had called last night and that you said you would still let us in this morning. What came next was a complete shock. The Pakistani Border Patrol, known famously as the "Khyber Riflemen" kindly explained that they have no phone line with the Afghani Patrol Border Guards. We had been totally played by the Afghani Guards. What came next was a total disbelief. Because from that day and for the next 30 days, all borders were closed entering into Pakistan due to the Islamic Conference and the security that had been ordered.

We were now struck in the Khyber Pass, stuck for 30 days in what is now known as one of the most dangerous places on this planet for a white Westerner. We could not return to Afghanistan without visas and we could not enter Pakistan. Even then being tribal one could not move more than a quarter of a mile radius on this border of no man's land. I would be living on peanuts, rice and green mint tea for the next 30 days. One hundred and fifty years ago, this is where a whole British regiment was ambushed and completely massacred, except for one soldier. We literally were there only under the protection of the famed Khyber Riflemen. I came to know this place as one of the most dangerous black markets in this world for guns, drugs, slave trade and black money.

About two weeks into our exile a British Diplomat showed up at the Khyber Pass border. It is a favored place where foreign diplomats would come to visit or bring guests to show off the famed Khyber Riflemen and the mountains of this famous place. His first question to us was, "What are you doing here?" We shared our story of being stuck here because of our expired visas and the borders being closed because of the Islamic Conference. He guaranteed he would get us out of there, for this was not a place to be stuck at.

Another week passed without hearing from the British diplomat again. But around the third week an American diplomat taking a tour of the Pass noticed we were here and asked us the same very question. He also said he would do whatever it took to get us out of here. Literally in two days the American diplomat had arranged visas for us to descend down the pass and reside in Peshawar in a guest house. We were told that we could stay the remaining week in Peshawar until the borders were opened and then we could transit through Pakistan. I suspect it must have been a safe house that was under the command of the US State Department. Who knew, but at least we were in a proper building with actual food instead of sleeping under the open sky with hardly anything to eat.

The caveat to this story was that we learned there was going to be a parade while we were stuck in Peshawar. We all decided to go and see who this important major leader was, which the parade was for. It turned out it was Colonel Muammar Gaddafi who had just taken control of Libya. This was 1973, and I stood watching less than 15 feet away as Colonel Gaddafi's open motorcar drove by. Until this day I can clearly see his face in my mind.

The Khyber Pass today is of course one of the most dangerous places be for a Westerner, back then it was dangerous in different ways for an American or European but still extremely dangerous for a non-Muslim to be stuck there. This is one of many stories that I look back upon and can consider as a character-building moment in my life. In this case of being trapped in the Khyber Pass for all those days, I learned to pay attention, show respect, and trust I will know the right action when called upon. The most significant thing I've learned is not to let fear dominate my thoughts and feeling so I can be clear to make the right decisions at the right times. Stay open and don't be quick to judge. Two powerful principles that have been true character builders for me all these years.

I crossed in to India on my 21st birthday in 1974. I giggle thinking that many of my friends on their 21st would be running to a bar to have their first legal alcoholic drink, while I was stepping into a mystical realm of magic and mystery half way around the world from home. As I shared previously, about my mystical experience with the white bearded saint in rags, there were many more stories like that one once I entered into India. I was once told by a Native American elder that many more miracles can happen in a culture that expects and accepts them versus our Western culture that does not give much credence or consider them to be real. This was for sure my experience. Often out of nowhere one would come up to me and know exactly what I was going through and help me find my way, either by pointing me in the right direction or imparting wisdom to this mystical world that saints and holy men of this country had expired, written and logged the pathways of.

I ended up living in India in a remote ashram in the southern rainforest of the Mysore Mountains for two years, meditating and living with the local tribal people. For India with its 10,000 years of spiritual history, I felt I finally understood what I was going through and could begin to answer the complexity of this inner world with the outer physical dimensions. I have continued to travel back to India these last 40 years on business, but more importantly I have come to know India as my second home: half American, half Indian in my soul. My Indian friends often comment on the fact I know more about their history and spirituality then they do.

Upon my return home from world travels, and after living in this remote monastery for almost two years I was lost as to what to do with my life.

So, I turned to art as a way to express my intelligence. But after discovering the art of gem carving I knew I had to learn the science behind the art. Gem Crystals were a wonder of the Earth and I wanted to know everything I could about my medium. I had never encountered an art that required so much science as the foundation. I had a very strong urge to return to college and learn about the material I was working with. I enrolled in courses such as Geology, Mineralogy, Chemistry and higher Mathematics to help me understand these rare natural substances that our Earth created that was the very medium of my art. Once back in college and interested in the subject I excelled in these courses because I had a deep passion and strong interest to understand these rare and exotic minerals that was the very medium I was creating with. All of a sudden math and science that eluded me as a child and teenager were now subjects that I found myself at the top of my class and deeply in touch with and intrinsically understood. As a child that could barely pass these courses in High School, I found myself maintaining a 3.95 grade point average in college. The mystical journey to the core of the atom became validated as I sat in classes and listened to my professors talk about this quantum world of the atom. I came to know my art medium intimately and understood the principles of light refraction, mineral formation and the physics and chemistry of crystallography. All of a sudden I was using both hemispheres of my brain. It was an art form like no other I had ever explored. I now felt that the questions that perplexed and eluded me were all coming together in some grand theory and that I had now found my destiny and purpose.

Gem cutting is a true synergy of Art and Science that has motivated and captivated my passion for all these decades. I eventually went on to get my degree in Gemology in residence from the Gemological Institute of America in 1978.

My travels proved to be one of those life-changing choices that set my course to a fulfilling career as an artist of gems and in life in general. It was my PhD university degree to life and the world of human relationships. The many different cultures and its people, I know I can look back on this period in my life as the Grand Theory of everything. My course was set and now I was to go about living the life of meaning we all feel propelled to find and discover. Living one's true purpose and destiny.

5

COMING TO MY ART

· The History of How I Discovered My Muse

"You can never change things by fighting the existing reality. To change something, build a new model that makes the existing model obsolete"
Buckminster Fuller

The Goddesses of the Muse, of which there are nine, were personified as knowledge of literature, arts, dance and music, and make up the pantheon of what is the symbolic essence of creativity. The pure, distilled meaning of finding one's Muse is when the knowledge of the science and art melt into one and can be seen as beauty and creative innovation. The ancient myth is Zeus (symbolic as the God source in Ancient Greek society) and Mnemosyne (one's personal memory) gave birth to nine daughters of creativity.

Symbolically, the number nine represents the individual becoming complete and whole within themselves; there is a wholeness and completion to one's level of fulfillment and enlightenment, according to my Basque teacher, the late

Angeles Arrien, PhD. When this state of consciousness is reached, one has a light that shines through them and out into the world as an inspiration and way to show others how to be inspired and discover their personal Muse. When I cut a gemstone, I feel the light that shines forth in the gemstones becomes a lasting inspiration for generations to come. I feel moved by this knowledge and remain constantly passionate to keep on creating.

To my mind, my concept of the Muses is manifested when I am open to inspiration from Nature or from our higher source of creation; my consciousness is ripe to receive new inspiration, new ideas and innovated concepts. When I studied the sciences that pertained to my craft as a Gem Carver, my level of understanding and the expression of my art took on a new level of creative expression. When I merged my knowledge of mineralogy, the years of practice in cutting gemstones along with years of mastering the arts in various mediums, my expression of Gem Art became exciting and innovative.

Buckminster Fuller was one of the greatest thinkers and inventors of the 20th century. He is most recognized for inventing the geodesic dome and coining the word Synergy in our modern vocabulary; simply stated as, "The combined parts of a whole are exponential greater than the sum of its parts." The Geodesic dome half-circle structure of interweaving triangles gives the physical form a very sturdy and solid foundation. This interweaving composition of triangles that completely mimic the structure of the Silicon Dioxide molecule, known in the gem world as Quartz, is one of the most stable if not the most stable solid form in nature. Buckminster Fuller took this molecular model and applied it to architecture. This series of interconnected equilateral triangles creates a perfect balance between tension and compression, creating a perfect solid form. The geodesic dome is so solid and stable it is used in the polar caps where winds can whip at 100-plus miles per hour on a daily basis. I was very lucky to have had a short but very fortunate opportunity to learn directly from him towards the end of his life. He was one of my mentors in the fields of science and innovation: a true renaissance man of the 20th century with a keen spiritual nature-based philosophy. What is spiritual nature? A Da Vinci in our life time.

After spending a couple of years in college studying geology, mineralogy and the macro world of crystallography, I could see how Nature drives towards perfection constantly. Even though you can't see this in the macro, it is a key to how all life builds itself from the chaos of the Big Bang. Later I will go more into the drive that all life from the atom to human is driven to this state of absolute balance and equilibrium.

The year was 1975. I had just returned to America from having traveled the world and living in a remote rain rainforest of Southern India for two and a half years in an ashram. In my travels and living overseas in a very foreign culture like India I saw parts of the world that could have been a scene in Rudyard Kipling novels: the giant mosques and bazaars of Turkey and Iran, the remote tribal village people of the Khyber Pass bordering Pakistan and Afghanistan along with the jungles, elephants and cobras of India. I was blown wide open. My understanding of my world was now completely inside out and upside down and I had not a single clue what I wanted to do with my life at the age of 23. I was searching for meaning and trying hard to make sense of how the world appears to be on the physical versus what I was experiencing in this hidden world. It was a journey into the world of paradoxes. Both were true but neither made sense on their own. I was searching to find the balance between the seen and unseen.

Upon returning home after the years of travel and living in foreign culture I was lost. I felt more disconnected and disoriented back in Los Angeles than I had in the remote rainforest of India. What I was raised to believe and know growing up in America and what I had come to experience through these paranormal mystical experiences and cultures of very foreign lands was a complete paradox and at opposite ends of understanding.

I was back in America living in San Francisco with my brother Wayne. I held a job at a restaurant as a dish washer. At the time, I was still going through the culture shock of coming back home and trying very hard to re-adjust to a life back in America. I had no clear direction to my life or what I wanted to do. I was in this liminal space where I could not go back to the way my life was before all this started on the inner level, yet I could not move forward because life in America seemed so materialistic and insignificant compared to where I'd been and what I had experienced in the past five years.

This is when it happened. In a single moment, when my older brother Wayne handed me this cut and polished piece of optical ice white Quartz. It was literally a lightning bolt of explosive energy in my mind and body. Because of my brother's simple act back then, when he placed that cut piece of optical Quartz in my hand, everything was set on a track with a lifetime of focus and manifestation. That

CUTS

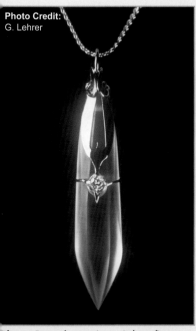

Above One of two pieces Lehrer first created back at the birth of his art. In this historic early photo is a frosted clear Quartz crystal cut in a soft obelisk shape, saddled with a Diamond and 14k yellow gold. Circa 1976.

Above A 107 ct hand carved and faceted flame style natural Madeira Citrine Quartz.

'Wings of Isis'
A hand carved, frosted optical clear Quartz with a faceted round brilliant Siberian Amethyst, set with Diamonds and 14k white and yellow gold. Circa 1982.

CO-DESIGNS

Above Three Gordon Aatlo designs using Lehrer TorusRing cuts. Left to right: **1.** Blue Sapphire with a Yellow Sapphire center in 18k yellow gold with Diamonds. **2.** Rhodolite Garnet with Diamonds set in 18k yellow gold. **3.** Chrome Tourmaline with Diamonds set in 18k yellow gold.

'Jinju
A Paula Crevoshay design
using a 100.8ct Lehrer
Fantasia carved Brazilian
Dendritic Agate

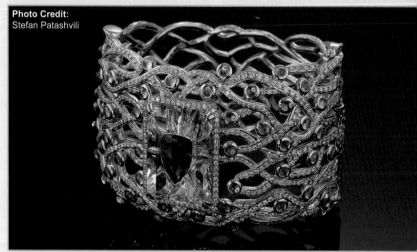

'Sentience'
Inspired by San Francisco's spirit of innovation, the Sentience bangle features a 7ct Deep Blue Pear-Shaped Tanzanite, invisibly set inside a 26ct cushion-cut Aquamarine TorusRing, accented with 6.19cts of Moonstones and 6.94cts of brilliant cut Diamonds in 18k white gold. Designed by Yehouda Saketkhou of Yael Designs. Gem design, carving and faceting by Lehrer.

CO-DESIGNS

Above A Kent Raible design using a
Tanzanite Lehrer TorusRing with Indicolite
bullet cabs, Diamonds and granulation
and fabricated 18k yellow gold.

Above A Kent Raible design using an
Afghani Bluish-Green Tourmaline marquise
shape Lehrer TorusRing, set with a faceted
Indicolite, Moonstone and granulation
hand fabricated 18k yellow gold.

'Ballerina' by Mark Schneider Designs,
using a Lehrer Fantasia carved Brazilian
banded clear Drusy and Carnelian Agate
with 18k yellow gold and Diamonds.

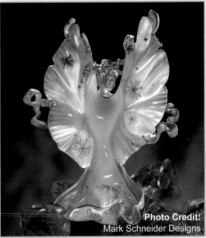

'Angel' by Mark Schneider Designs,
using a Lehrer Fantasia carved
Brazilian Dendritic Agate with 18k
yellow gold and Diamonds.

IDAR-OBERSTEIN

Above Lehrer's first major carving in Idar-Oberstein, with master carver Bernard Becker. Lehrer carved the frosted clear Quartz orchid flower and Becker carved the Chrysoprase hummingbird in the 'Plastik' technique, perfected in the Idar valley over centuries. Circa 1987.

'Dreaming of Palenque' by Glenn Lehrer and Bernard Becker. This was the first in a series of sculptures innovated by Lehrer where he explored creating reflections of knowable images, such as this women's face in a highly refracted natural large gemstone. This style would eventually be called Visionary GemArt, that Lehrer innovated and co-designed with Becker. Features a carved and faceted natural Deep Yellow Citrine with 18k yellow gold and a black slate base. Circa 1991.

Above The Felsenkirche (Chapel in the Rocks) church, carved into the mountainside in Idar-Oberstein, dates back to 1482. A natural, vividly bubbling spring flows from the rock into the chapel.

Above Right Glenn Lehrer trying out the original method of lapidary used in Idar Oberstein, Germany, in the 1800s. While lying down, facing a sandstone grinding wheel powered by water, the lapidarist worked in this position for hours. It is by no means a comfortable method for cutting stone. This studio is apparently the last privately owned, original waterwheel lapidary studio powered in the old fashion way. Just over a 100 years ago, in the valley, there were hundreds of cutting studios like this one. In the photo, on the right side, the stove barrel with a chimney pipe is used to heat the cold stone walled studio and is also where the lapardist heats the acid to dye Agate different colors. A very old method of enhancement.

IDAR-OBERSTEIN

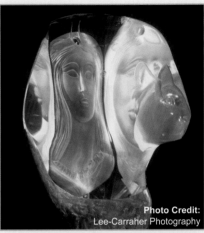

'The Sun Temple' by Lehrer-Pauly Visionary GemArt. This piece was featured on the cover of Lapidary Journal, February 1996. It features a 4,100ct natural Brazilian Golden Yellow Citrine Quartz, measuring 15.2x7.1x4.5cm. With a black marble base and 14k yellow gold, the sculpture stands at 39cm. The Citrine was faceted so that when the intaglio of the temple is carved in the back, one can see through the front table of stone five different images of the temple. Thus it is truly visionary. Circa 1995.

'Cat Women' by Lehrer-Pauly Visionary GemArt. A very large 16,350ct optically clear Quartz, measuring 20.5x16.0x10.5cm, faceted and carved by intaglio with a bronze base. The women is carved from the back and is then reflected from the back side. The cat is a carved cameo on the front. Circa 1996.

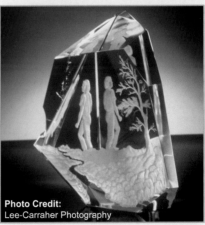

Above Hans Ulrich "Uli" Pauly and Glenn Lehrer at the Getty Museum in Los Angeles, California doing one of their favorite things. Looking at art, when they are not busy carving together. Circa 1996.

'The Wanderer' by Lehrer-Pauly Visionary GemArt. A very large optically clear Quartz with thin zones of Citrine and Smoky Quartz, weighing approximately 20,000cts and measuring 17.9x18.7x11.4cm. Faceted and carved by intaglio. Circa 1995.

BAHIA

Above Lawrence Stoller (left) and Glenn Lehrer (right) straddle Bahia in its rough state, with the wire saw above, when Bahia was about to have her first cut and facet. The original piece weighed 800lbs (363.6kgs). **Origin:** Bahia, Brazil. Circa 1989.

Above Lehrer and Stoller, after removing the clay rough surface from Bahia, saw that two natural cleavage planes were revealed. They had been hidden under the original clay surface. This is after a few 'Ah-Ha' moments and wondering, "What are we going to now that it's clear we can't have one large sculpture?" After some time, the new vision of Bahia transformed into a hanging necklace with 3 pieces, held together and suspend by gold plated steel.

Above Lawrence Stoller and Glenn Lehrer at the then Soviet Peace Committee Ministry exhibit of nuclear disarmament between the USA and the former USSR. The **'Empress Crystal'** was the center focus of a public exhibit at the Ministry in Moscow. Stoller and Lehrer loaned it to the Russian Academy of Natural Sciences in Moscow as part of a cultural exchange between the USA and the former USSR. It was during the period know as Perestroika and Glasnost between the two countries. Circa 1989.

BAHIA

'The Empress of Lemuria'
A 42lb, natural optical White Quartz crystal. The very first of its kind anywhere in the world. Circa 1986.

Photo Credit:
Harold and
Erica Van Pelt

Photo Credit:
Harold and
Erica Van Pelt

Stoller and Lehrer standing side by side with the completed Bahia. It weighs 425lbs (193.3kgs, approximately 1,000,000cts).

SCULPTURE

Photo Credit:
Jeff Scovil

Photo Credit:
Lee-Carraher
Photography

Above A large sculptured Dendritic Drusy Agate as part of the **'Dancing Angel'** series. Now in a private collection, it was on display at the Carnegie Museum.

'Kalahari Encounter'
A very large, carved, fantasy-style Smoky Citrine with a black granite sculptured neckline base.

ONE-OF-A-KINDS

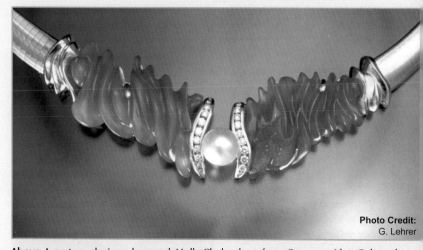

Above A custom designed, carved, Holly Chalcedony from Oregon with a Cultured Pearl, Diamond and set in 18k yellow gold.

'Man in the Moon'
A hand carved, frosted Quartz set with a hanging Emerald, inlayed Opal and a trillion Diamond, set in 18k yellow gold. Circa 1995.

'Toucan Sam'
Custom designed and fabricated by Paul Klecka for the Chicago Zoo charity event. Features Lehrer carved pieces of Amethyst, Pink Tourmaline, Orange Fire Opal and, for the eye, Paraiba Tourmaline with Diamond. Done like pieces of a puzzle, the stones are like carved intarsia mosaic.

started the revolution and journey that has led to a life time of adventure and discovery. This simple act started the journey, discovery and ultimate mastery into the world of minerals and Gem Artistry. A self-guided, self-taught apprenticeship to becoming a gemstone artist that completed this circle that my inner metaphysical world had first given me a glimpse into five years earlier. I found my medium of art in life, a career and big piece of my destiny. All the parts were in place for the synergy to happen. My metaphysics desired to express this rich inner world: the science that held the solid foundation was the best way to communicate it and the art was the ultimate vision of the indescribable states I had experienced in previous years. Indescribable in that the light and color natural gemstones give back to us along with the emotions they ignite in our hearts was the first physical form and art that came the closest to what I had seen and felt in these deeper states of consciousness.

Back in 1976 when I first began to explore and discover gem carving in America, where there is little to no history of the craft of gem cutting - unlike Europe and Asia - there existed no school or master where one could study and learn this craft. Of course, one could learn faceting or cabochon cutting from a gem and mineral society club but I was not interested in this and it held no fascination for me at the time. There were gem cutting houses in New York, but for the most part held very secretly within a family that had migrated from Europe in the late 19th and early 20th century. There was no opportunity to learn from a master of the craft I so enthusiastically wanted to delve into. Venturing into the field of gem carving was a new horizon and an uncharted medium of art I knew nothing about. I knew at the time there was nobody to turn to even for answers to simple questions about equipment and tools.

Eventually, I stumbled into this field by sheer fate and luck. It was not my karma to be born into a family of jewelry and I had no real knowledge or understanding of field gemology and the medium of Gem Art. As a teenager and young man I was an artist who explored the many mediums of art from oil painting, sculpture, photography and graphic arts. Gemstones and jewelry held no particular draw at the time. I didn't simply want to know how to cut a cabochon, I wanted to know how to carve and sculpt a gemstone, given my background of being more of a fine artist. Looking around in America for a teacher would be fruitless because there was almost no tradition and those that knew were not at all interested in teaching unless you were a family member. So, I went out and bought my first lapidary equipment and began to experiment and explore the art. My initial purchase included a saw, a 6" cabbing machine and a flexible shaft hand piece and thus my gemstone carving began.

Looking back now, they were crude tools but were the only one's offered for sale, plus I didn't have a clue which were the best tools anyway. I was flying outside the box in a medium that I had not a clue as to what the boundaries were. Later in this book I will focus on the equipment and tools used in a modern Gem Artist Studio, but this is a world apart from where I started. Because I was without a teacher for the first ten years I had no idea what one could or should do with a gemstone. I was functioning in a complete bubble and unchartered world of artist exploration. Looking back, I can see in many ways this was a gift. It gave me complete freedom to create without the confines of age old apprenticeship traditions, handed down from generation to generation. There is this fine line for me when I learn a skill that's been in use for several generations and breaking outside the box and looking for a completely unique and new way of approaching a technique. Just because it's been done one way does not often mean there's not a better way. I believe there is a fine line in taking in what has been, maximizing the knowledge but always remaining open and humble to the possibility there's a better way, i.e. quicker execution time, better technique or a superior water clear polish. To this day I am always learning something new in my field of expertise. My principle here is, "Stay open to new ideas and be willing to change."

As I began my exploration into this unique and unknown art form I had no restrictions on what I could do or not do with gemstone material. I thus began to teach myself stepping into a completely uncharted territory. I would dream an image, go to work with my rotary hand piece and carve away.

The hardest technique I had to learn on my own was getting that water clear polish. Essential for turning any gemstone in to a true gem; polish is everything. This took me years to perfect. A side story I need to share to further elaborate this is as follows. It was ten years into my career when I first went to Idar-Oberstein, Germany, to meet the fabled land of Gem Art and the living masters, after working within a bubble of isolation for many years, self-teaching, experimenting and totally free for self-creative exploration. The first group of master cutters I met in Idar-Oberstein in 1986 couldn't believe I had cut and polished the stones on my own, without a teacher, plus they would say, "How do you get your polish?" Later in the book I will share more about my travels to and the subsequent years in Idar as an outsider who was allowed in past the closed studio doors to work alongside several living masters of the craft.

I have a very strong philosophy as an artist that if it has been done before I'm not interested in doing it. I have followed this quote throughout my whole professional artist career, "If it has been done before, it is not art. Inspiration alone belongs altogether to the individual; everything else, including skill, can now be acquired by anyone. Inspiration remains the only factor in the creation of a successful work of art that cannot be copied or imitated". Clement Greenberg, New York art critic, in his essay 'After Abstract Expressionism', first published in Art International, VI, no.8, October 1962.

Copying for me has never been art, but simply studying and learning techniques of another master. Once I learn the techniques from studying another's artistry, then finding my own original design is the zenith for me becoming a true master of my craft. What is truly difficult - and I believe I owe my success to is - out of one's imagination of originality and beauty there can emerge inspiration that others can feel and be inspired by.

I stumbled into the field where I had no rules that I had to follow or no craftsmen guild that closely guarded the art. It was a wide open art form where I taught myself the craft. I learned my craft in an isolated world for the first ten years. The techniques I developed and styles I created were simply a process of trial and error on my own. You might say I paid for my education in the early days by my mistakes and loss of precious material.

Living and creating in a vacuum meant I could do whatever I wanted and come up with techniques that were and are completely novel to the craft even to this day. Having been self-taught also meant that I could do things in gem material that had not been explored before. I have a very strong philosophy that whatever I create should be completely novel and unique to the field of Gem Artistry. This is how, after almost 40 years in the field, I have come to be known as one who creates Gem Art outside the box, such the creation of Bahia and the original TorusRing gem cut (for which I was awarded a US utility patent for this unique invention in gem cutting).

One of my drives is to constantly create and think outside the box. Sometimes it can appear that no one understands where one is coming from but eventually the physical world just needs to catch up with one's ideas or thinking because one is just ahead of his or her time. I often refer to this as the "Jet Lag of Life" effect. It's possible that when one feels out of place or misunderstood, it can mean you are just ahead of the curve and the rest around you need to catch up with a new model or way to live. To me, this can reflect that one is thinking outside the box; one has just moved their sense of reality to a whole new level and dimension. Helping in small or large ways in having lasting impact on humanity. A never-ending and constant evolution of life on this planet that has moved humanity forward in beliefs and attitudes as to what it means to be human.

The real beauty to me now after 40 years as a Gem Artist is I have never tired of or lost my passion to create with gemstones. From the date I cut my first gemstone so many years ago until today, I still get that "wow!" factor after I finish a polish on a gemstone that I've cut and created. To me, this is the very essence of being bathed in my Muse: the awe and wonder of beauty and creativity flowing effortlessly through me.

I have the same passion and drive today, since the very first day of cutting. I just can't wait to see what lies ahead in my creative expression. I feel like after 40 years I have just hit my stride and feel my best work lies ahead of me.

6

WHAT IT TAKES TO BE A GEMSTONE ARTIST

· A Short Historical View of the Art

*"The Love of Gemstones is deeply
planted in the human heart."*
George Frederick Kunz (1856-1932)
Renowned gem expert for Tiffany & Co

I am very excited to open a unique window and personal perspective into this rare art form that has been held as a secret for centuries by those who have worked, traded and sold gemstones.

I can only speak from the Western standpoint of Gem Art because there is a long and very rarified existence even older than Europe of Gem Art in the Orient that dates back for centuries in Jade carving. I will not go into the Oriental history of the art which is beyond my knowledge, except for a minor understanding of the lineage of the art in the East. I also have no intention of giving the definitive view on Western Europe's role in the history of Gem Art, just a brief overview of Gem Art as I have come to understand it today in the dawn of the 21st century here in the United States and Europe.

This chapter is only intended to give a very brief overview as to the history and short description in my own personal interpretation of what the terms "Gem Art" and "Gem Artist" mean. So new is the term Gem Art that I believe there is no real definition for the word that has come into use in modern times. I believe the word Gem Art is a very recent term applied to artists like myself that came of age in the late 20th century and the many more who now practice the art in the beginning of the 21st century. There are numerous books that have been written on lapidary, gem cutting and basic tools but very little has been printed about this new genre in the world of gem cutting. Gem Art could in a wide definition mean the art of carving, sculpting and cutting gemstones in new and exciting ways not seen before in the field of lapidary. This could be seen as the creative animal carvings that Idar-Oberstein is so famous for that was brought to a zenith during the era of Faberge (1846-1920), and the modern and very stylized cameo carvings that someone like Erwin Pauly brought to the public, starting back in the 1950s and 1960s. More recently the term 'fantasy cuts' - a form of carving into the stone negative cuts that reflect and refract with very defined flat facets organized to reflect these negative cuts (innovated by Bernd Munsteiner of Idar, circa early 1970s) - which helped create a whole new genre in cutting. Although it is often referred to as "Laser Cutting", this is actually a misnomer, it is in fact very carefully done by hand the old fashioned way with grinding wheels.

I would say the very first wave of the art in the Western

world, and most specifically in Europe in gemstone material that can still be seen today that was created was during the Renaissance period (14th-16th centuries). One can visit numerous museums and castles of Europe and see this fabulous art of gem material on display. Sacred religious Gem Art and vessel style bowls and cups in gem material commissioned by the royal families of the day and the church itself. These were the patrons of the day that fostered this craft. Since signing this type of art back then was not allowed or even considered possible like a painting or marble sculpture, we have no records as to whom these masters of the day were. They are lost to antiquity.

The next big period as an emergence of what I would call Gem Art was during Faberge's period which then continued on into the Art Nouveau period with artists like Rene Lalique and Tiffany, and then into the Art Deco period with extraordinary Gem Art with major jewelry houses like Cartier. World War II had a devastating impact on Gem Art in the villages of Idar-Oberstein, Germany; many of the young carvers were scripted into the war, or those in the very large Jewish community of the gem business were either sent to concentration camps or labor camps. I was told by a local in Idar that many of the very best Jewish carvers were sent to labor camps where they were made to carve and fabricate the medals for the German Army. Idar did not recover until the mid-1950s, from what I was told.

During all these periods in history, going back to Roman times, the actual craftsmen would receive little or no recognition. This whole concept of the artist signing his/her work in Gem Art did not start until masters like Erwin Pauly, the renowned master cameo carver from Idar-Oberstein, started the practice in the 1950s and 1960s. He personally told me how in those days they criticized him in the Idar valley for doing this at the time. I am not sure, but his teacher Richard Hahn, who is credited with bringing back cameo carving to Idar-Oberstein after the war, may have actually started the practice. Most Gem Artists throughout history have passed on without any real recognition as to whom the creator was. For centuries, this craft was closely guarded and the doors to a lapidary studio closed unless you were invited in to apprentice with a master of this craft. Most guild crafts in Europe were passed on from within one's family or taught by a master to his or her chosen apprentices if found to show some adept ability in this rare medium of art. These skills and techniques were closely guarded and considered extremely rare at the heart of this precious art form and kept a deep secret in centuries past.

In times of old it would not be easy for an outsider to even consider a career as a lapidarist due to a large extent of the preciousness and rarity of the material, coupled with skills that can take years to perfect. Until just recently even the craftsmen of lapidary were hidden from the public eye, and their art was brought out into the world by a gem dealer who made sure no one knew the artist or creator. This was the asset of the gem dealer who kept others from knowing the creator/artist of the gemstone. I realize I have a grand opportunity in the 21st century to open wide the doors to my art studio and share this mysterious secret world of gem cutting and Gem Art. In the next chapter I will go into a bird's eye view of a working Gem Art studio with a brief outline of tools and basic techniques to create this exacting art form.

The craft is not an easy art to learn from a master, let alone being self-taught. In the past, being self-taught was completely unheard of. There were a handful of unknown cutters in the US, of which I am one, who back in the 1970s and early 80s labored in obscurity, through trial and error, to master this art, unlike many in the guild schools of Europe. This included Henry Hunt, considered the grandfather of American Gem Artists. It was not until I met Henry Hunt in a jewelry store in San Francisco around 1977 did I know anyone else even thought and carved like I did. Later in my career I learned about Francis Sperisen (1900-1986) who lived right in my backyard in San Francisco. Unfortunately, I did not know of him at the time. A real master of lapidary who did very unusual work for his day, back in 1940-1960s. His work can be seen today in museums, set in modernist style silver jewelry by very creative designers during the Beat Generation in the USA. He was truly a trailblazer in the history of American Gem Artistry.

Others of my generation as the first major wave of American Gem Artists from the mid 70s through the 90s that came to public attention are Steve Walters, whose family was in the business; Michael Dyber, another innovator working in isolation like myself; and the late Arthur Anderson to name just a few. We were the first wave of Gem Artists from America. At this point in time I was completely unaware of the tradition or major masters of the day in Idar-Oberstein such as Erwin Pauly, master cameo carver; his son and my very good friend Hans Ulrich Pauly; Bernd Munsteiner; considered the grandfather of fantasy carving, and Manfred Wild, master of the sculptures and objects. The knowledge of these German Masters' very existence did not come to me until 1986, 11 years after I had started carving away in obscurity without a mentor.

Later in the book I will share more about a short history of Idar-Oberstein, where I found myself at the doorsteps of many Masters in this small village in Germany. But first, I want to share a short history as I have come to understand from the 1970s onward to this new level of Gem Art that has come into existence first in Germany and the USA, and now has worldwide acceptance in the gem and jewelry industry, along with a huge public demand now in the 21st century. Currently, many of my colleagues and myself feel we are living an epic moment in the history of Gem Art and Jewelry, akin to the periods of the Renaissance, Edwardian, Art Nouveau and Art Deco times in history. We are living in a time in history that others in the future will look back on as a revolutionary change in the use of gemstone material and a genius moment in jewelry designs.

It was not until the middle to late part of the 20th century that the actual artist/lapidary craftsperson in Europe and US began to promote themselves and sign their work. Just recently for the first time in history, the world was able to come to know the artist behind the work. As I have mentioned, for the Gem Artist to even sign his or her work was frowned upon until just a few decades ago. For centuries, many pieces of the finest Gem Art have been left anonymous forever, lost to the chronicles of time and history. Even in the late 19th and early 20th century the great works from houses such as Tiffany, Cartier and Faberge, the actual craftsman were often never given full credit for their skill. These great houses of jewelry and gemstone designs would come with their ideas to the lapidarist and have them execute the actual work. I remember a German carver friend and colleague opening a Faberge book on gem art and showing me pictures of great works credited to the House of Faberge and explaining that his grandfather did this piece and their great uncle carved this work as a commission.

It was not until the middle of the 20th century that some of the finest Gem Artists from Germany began to sign their own work, along with the few of us recognized from America. In the beginning, when these Master Gem Artists of the mid-20th century started this practice of self-promotion and signing their own work, the industry strongly criticized them for doing so. It was the start of how the businessman could no longer keep these highly trained masters from the world knowing who they were. Now there are several like myself who create and self-promote; and the jewelry designers who use our work acknowledge us as the creator of the Gem Art in their designs. As a matter of fact, nowadays, when a designer's brand acknowledges the use of gemstone components by a well-known Gem Artist, it increases the perceived value of the design.

We are living in an era now where the art and craft is fully recognized and appreciated for who created it and what it is. There was a whole new Renaissance that came into existence in the late 1970s and is now in full swing in the 21st century with a huge array of styles and techniques of carving and cutting gemstones. There has now been a second and third wave of new individuals since I started, now working in the field creating exciting new designs in Gem Art. A period in the history of jewelry design where the designer of the metal work acknowledges and gives credit for the Gem Art incorporated into their work. We're living in very exciting times that I hope will be definitively recorded in the long history of Gem Art throughout human history. I am deeply satisfied to know I was one of the forbearers back in the late 70s and 80s to help birth the craft and bring it to a high degree of public awareness today as to its actual existence. It's the dream of any artist during his or her lifetime to leave their mark in their chosen art medium. I can proudly look back on my body of work up to this point and know I've hit my mark when it comes to being a living successful artist.

7

THE STUDIO OF
A GEM ARTIST

· A Sneak Peak at Centuries Held Secrets
· A Bird's Eye View of the Lehrer Studio

How does a kid from Los Angeles with no family background, training or apparent access to the resources become a renowned Gem Artist worldwide? On the surface, there is no logic to the story. Below the surface, it's in my imagination and a never-ending perseverance at keeping at it, piece-by-piece, step-by-step, building experience and knowledge, I can look back now after 40 years and see how I arrived at this place. With this intense personal perseverance and drive, along with the many ups and downs in the early years as a Gem Artist, I never took "no" as the final answer from the so-called experts and business people of our trade to something I felt so strong about. I felt and knew in my heart I would eventually succeed at it.

There was major resistance to new or innovative cutting; the industry did not understand what I started to introduce and promote back in the 80s and even through the 90s. A great example to this was the TorusRing cut, invented back in 1998. For at least the first three to four years I would hear from experts such as goldsmiths or jewelry manufacturers, "How do you set the stone?" or, "What to do with the hole in the center?", this was a constant in the day that I repeatedly had to talk through and coach these so-called experts to experiment and try something new like the TorusRing cut. I will talk more about the invention of the TorusRing later, but my point here is often how the very experts in the field can be the most resistant. Though I enjoyed some relatively small success with the TorusRing within the industry of designer jewelers and boutique manufactures, I could not get the majors in our industry to try and promote in a massive way. For over 12 years I would try and promote the concept of the cut to the industry, only to constantly come in contact with resistance and reasons why not. That was until I met Steve Bennett in 2011 and he saw something he knew was extraordinarily unique in a gemstone style and felt he could promote it; that TorusRing cut went global to where in four years we've sold well in excess of 60,000 pieces worldwide. The TorusRing cut is now a household name with fine jewelry connoisseurs worldwide.

"Show up, pay attention and do the right thing." This is my mantra for gem cutting and even more importantly, the principles I live my life by. Now after 40 years my addition to these three key principles to being a Gem Artist and the living of life to its fullest is, "Often the least amount of effort can create the greatest effect". In plain English, it could be termed as 'elegance', the quality of ease and ingeniousness in one act.

"To Show Up" means to be present, focused and aware of

where I am at that very moment. For gem cutting it means I need to be 100% present to start the work. To work on this natural, very rare medium that has been on this planet for at least 40 million years I better show up, pay attention and then do the right thing. To meditate on this concept that this very rare natural substance lay dormant in the Earth's deep caverns for millennia forces me to show up and be conscious that I am about to transform this rare mineral into an object for beauty that will live for generations to come. The sense of responsibility I feel every time I cut a gemstone is immense. I need to be present and aware of my actions before I start carving away on this very real and rare object. I take this on as a very great responsibility every time I step up to the cutting wheel. This mantra is also so true to one's life journey. One thing I've learned in life is that we often go through the motions in life but are not always that present or aware of the moment we are standing in at that very time and place. So, like gem cutting, I can see how showing up at every moment and being present for that person or situation is what calls forth 100% personal attention.

"Pay Attention" means to give my 100% attention to the moment and actions I'm undertaking in the present. That means not thinking or feeling something from the past or where I'm going later in the future. So often our mind wonders and is not fully paying attention to the action we're going through at that very moment in time. If one's mind wanders for just a second during the cutting, everything can quickly go very wrong and major mistakes can happen that one cannot recover from. So, if I'm not feeling just right, anxious, stressed or just in a funk then I should not sit down at the cutting bench. Over the years I've learned to know and sense if I'm in the right space to be working on something so precious as gem material. This often does not go well with my gem customers, because they want their stone tomorrow and if I'm not in the right head space then I have to continue to excuse myself from their work. It's a balance between doing the right thing, making my customer happy and listening to my inner whispers as to where I am in mind, body and emotion.

"Do the Right Thing" to me means that each gem rough has a destiny as well as we do in life. So often in life we do what others expect of us or what we think others want of us for approval. In gem cutting, so many gemstones are cut for their commercial value, forced into calibrated shapes without any consideration given to what a precious rough natural gemstone may want. You ask, "How could a gemstone want something, it's just an inanimate object?" I would beg to differ. They cannot walk or verbally talk, but if one's inner voice is in tune with them and one listens closely they can tell you what the best evolution is for them. One of my mantras as a Gem Artist is, "This mineral has been lying dormant in the Earth for millions of years, I'm just about to be the one who transforms it from what it has been to what it will be for centuries to come. I need to do the right thing by it. It's my responsibility to show up, listen and act in the right way."

I also personally see it as my duty to responsibly transfer the ownership of Nature's treasures.

To work and live by the principle of, "Often the least amount of effort can create the greatest effect" has come with years of passionate practice in my chosen art form. I've long done my 10,000 hours the experts say is needed to master a skill. So it's not without great effort and several small failures along the way that I can now just relax, observe, determine the best plan of action and then in the least amount of time create some of my most intricate gemstone carvings.

Once one has truly mastered their craft or field of expertise, then the fun begins. Every action is elegant and done with ease. There is less experimenting and groping in the dark to find that magic. I'm now at a place in my life and art, if I can imagine it, I can create it and live it.

Another principle I contemplate is the issue of right or wrong in one's actions. The origin of "sin" is an ancient Greek word "hamartia". Before it was interpreted by the New Testament in the Bible to mean having done bad or evil in one's life, it actually meant whether one in archery hit their mark or not. My Basque teacher, the late Angeles Arrien, PhD. used to say, "There is not right or wrong in one's life. It's whether you hit your mark or not." Then I would add "With harm to no one." Harm means it has repercussions; in Hindi they call it Karma. As one of my dear Indian friends and business colleagues would say, "My children's children will owe your family if I cause you harm for the next three generations out." Like in life, in Gem Art you have really only one chance. You can't put back what you've taken away. So it is critical to be sure every act is done with complete focus and attention. Gem Art is a precise art with very strong governing rules. This can be completely the opposite to, let's say, laying paint on canvas that can be free and uninhibited. In Gem Art one needs to know the hardness of the material, its crystal habit, its angles of refraction if transparent, placement of inclusions, and characteristics such as cleavage or brittleness. Only with mindfulness can one form something of true beauty that can capture the natural splendor and light that lays dominate until a Gem Cutter does his or her magic.

To be a Gem Artist, I have often said that one needs to be an artist, a machinist and have a basic background in the sciences of mineralogy and gemology. One also needs the ability to evaluate gem rough for yield in weight in combination with determining the best finished shape of the rough. This skill plays most importantly in the ability to make or literally break you financially due to the high value of the material. This aspect of lapidary is very difficult and takes years to master. It is the skill between making a beautifully valued gemstone or losing lots of money and ending up with only dust going down the drain. It should be noted not all gemologists understand rough, and not all Master Cutters or carvers are gemologists. But having a background in mineralogy and gemology does give one a greater understanding of the medium one is working with.

It is a unique art form that requires a blend of creativity, basic understanding of your machinery and the science of mineralogy and the physics of light refraction. A synergy so powerful I have never discovered it for myself in any other art medium.

Not all lapidary techniques are the same. There is the skill of faceting which means that you place a series of flat polished surfaces in a geometric pattern on a transparent gemstone within the critical angle of that gem material in order to reflect and refract light. Then there is cutting a cabochon which is a domed rounded surface often in transparent to opaque gem material. And finally, to be a carver or cameo engraver which is the most difficult of lapidary skills. As soon as one goes from doing flat surfaces in faceting and convex round surfaces on a cabochon to negative engraved carving, the skill level jumps tenfold. Along with this, as soon as one goes concave into a stone it takes five times longer to achieve a polish in a negative surface. Even within carving there are degrees of techniques, such as cameo, intaglio (reversed carving versus cameo which is raised) and finally, carving actual mini-sculptures. Each of these skills require years to master. If one goes to a school in Europe and studies with a Master, the program takes eight years to complete and receive one's Master Diploma.

Being self-taught I found this to be true in that it took me approximately eight years to master the many skills and learn the different techniques of cutting and carving with different gemstone material. After the first eight years, it seemed to take me approximately a further seven or eight years to explore my artistic style and to freely create what my imagination could conjure up. Having shared this observation with Master Carvers in Idar-Oberstein, many shared the same experience of 14 to 16 years before coming into their own style and mastery.

Mind you, one can learn the basics in a year or so. But to be able to master the many techniques and work with a wide array of different colored gemstones which require different carving, sanding, polishing tools and techniques; this is where the years of experience is required. It is about on par with one going through a higher education to receive a PhD in one's chosen field.

What Tools Make up a Gem Artist's Studio?

This can vary from Artist to Artist depending on his or her given focus and creativity. I am more of a jack of all trades that happens to really excel in the field of fluid carving so my studio seems to have almost all the necessary tools for various levels of carving, faceting and drilling.

Starting with the carving machine after realizing I could not go on carving forever with a flex shaft style rotary hand piece, I knew I needed to transfer over to what is known as a fixed arbor spindle. I was in the process of making one from scratch when I ventured to the tiny village of Idar-Oberstein, where 500 years of perfecting the arbor specifically for gem carving and engraving seemed good enough for me! I purchased one high speed precision Fortuna spindle, state of the art in 1986 for cameo and animal carving in Idar and one double shaft Babbitt style spindle for heavy carving and grinding. Both spindles after 30 years are still running strong and as true in my studio today as they were back then. Ten years later I added a very small, fine single shaft Babbitt spindle used in Idar-Oberstein for cameo intaglio carving. This style spindle still used today by carvers goes back several hundred years. The only difference today is we have motors: back then it was either apprentice labor hand cranking the wheel, water-wheel power or a treadle style pedaling, similar to the pre-electric sewing machines.

I have no idea how the phrase "Gem Cutting" came into use. Sounds good, but the fact is one does not cut stone like bread or wood; one grinds away. The physics is impossible with the possible exception of using high power water jet guns, but then you're still doing the same physics a "cutter" does, which is; you grind! Its high-power water stream wears away the surface like millennia of alluvial water wear you often see on many of gem rough pieces from around the world.

And the "laser cutting" that people always ask me about is

actually a huge misnomer in gemstones. It is just not that feasible in colored gemstones because of heat sensitivity. When I use what we call a round circular Diamond saw you are still grinding away as thin as it may appear. It's all about grinding to varying degrees and then finer and finer sanding particles until you reach the polish in that particular gemstone.

Every gemstone has its favorite method of grinding, sanding and polishing. Diamond has become the superior abrasive particularly in most cases for grinding and sanding. Then to achieve a polish, one can use Diamond or a group of oxide powders such as cerium and aluminum oxide. This is one of the longest learning curves in being a Master in gem cutting: learning and achieving a water fine polish in an array of many different colored gemstone materials. The difference between Diamond cutting and all other gemstones is, Diamond cuts all colored gems, but the only abrasive to cut Diamond is another Diamond.

I will not get into faceting or cabbing since there are is plenty of literature on these subjects, but so little is out there for the professional let alone the public on the subject of carving and the tools needed.

One of the most important tools in a Gem Carver's studio is the stationary spindle that holds your Diamond tools to carve, sand and polish with. When I first began back in 1976 I did not even know a machine like this existed. I started with what is called a flexible rotary shaft with motor used virtually by every jeweler around the world. It is a variable speed motor with a long flexible shaft and a handheld hand piece with a Jacobs chuck to hold the tools. There are several limitations to carving with this type of machine. Though it is great for doing very, very detailed work in small sizes it has other shortcomings. First, when working on larger size carvings like I do, one is constantly hitting up against the stone with the chuck portion of the hand piece. Basically, you need a really wide clearance when doing some very complicated style carving that I often do in my Fantasia Style Chalcedony carvings and my large objects of art.

Another limitation with this style of carving is one hand is holding the hand-piece with the Diamond but the other hand is holding the gemstone material. I find a lack of control with a hand-piece style coupled with the stress my wrist would encounter from the years of carving would affect the longevity I have enjoyed in carving all these years. A real shortcoming to the rotary hand-piece is that the further the tool extended, the greater the chance the Diamond tool would not run dead true and wobble. Wobble in your Diamond tool is deadly in that the chatter in the tool can easily damage the stone, plus it makes it extremely difficult to do any really fine detail.

Another limitation is the hand-piece can only hold certain types of tools in length and diameter of bur size, whereas a stationary spindle can hold virtually any size, type or shape of tool - from the finest, smallest size bur to very large in diameter carving tools.

And lastly, a flex shaft style carving is much slower in execution for a multiple of reasons than using a fixed arbor style. Mostly because with a fixed arbor one can hold the stone with both hands and have freedom to rotate the stone in virtually all angles to the wheel. This is paramount in being able to create a beautiful carving in a reasonable time period, so the end result is still within what the industry is willing to pay. Mind you, if you're a hobbyist you can take all the time in the world. But as a professional I am mindful of the clock for what I can realize for my work or when I am being commissioned by a professional jeweler or gem dealer there is only so much they are willing to pay for the work at hand.

The fix arbor spindles I have employed in my studio were purchased from Idar-Oberstein where they have been engineered and perfected over centuries. At the time in 1986 I knew I needed to evolve past the flex shaft style and was researching how I could make my own type of fix arbor spindle because there was none readily available that I could purchase in America. But once I ventured into the valley of Idar and was invited to work alongside some of the greatest living Masters I quickly realized I did not need to re-invent the wheel all over again.

I now have three very distinct types of spindles in my studio. The high-speed style Fortuna brand, that back in those days sold in the thousands just for the spindle housing. It is a very complex multiple closed bearing type with a long extended shaft that allows a long reach and absolutely no wobble or vibration at the end of the attached Diamond tool. These types of heavy duty bearing housings are what are commonly used on very heavy duty mill machines in a tool and die metal machine shop. The cost of this type of spindle does not include the large direct drive variable speed motor, the table its mounted on or the water catch pan that is required.

The other two spindles I have in my studio are what are called Babbitt style spindles. They are also made in Idar-Oberstein, and the design of these types have not changed for centuries. I have seen some antique versions that some of my friends' great-grandfathers used, over 120 years ago. The only difference then was either they were powered by treadle foot peddling or the many water wheels that were used to generate power for centuries, versus today's modern electrical motors with variable speed control. This ancient type of spindle goes back centuries. It does not have any ball bearings common in today's modern bearing house type spindles, but instead is an arbor shaft that rests in a lead-formed housing around the shaft and is lubricated by oil. The beauty of this style spindle is that they can always run true versus the bearing style, which when it is running out of true I've had to take it to a machinist to rebuild a couple of times over my 35+ years working with it. With a Babbitt style, all I need to do is adjust the carriage screws that house the shaft around the lead and the spindle runs true as I need it to.

I have two of these types of spindles in my studio. Each has a very specific purpose. One is a double shaft with a left and right side that I use for heavy duty grinding and carving and can hold the heavy weight often associated with large steel sintered Diamond wheels. They can also handle the torque at low speeds when grinding really tough material like Chalcedony, Agate or Jade. The beauty as well for this type of spindle is it can also perform perfectly if you're running a very small fine carving bur point and have it run dead true with no wobble. I have employed this very spindle in my workshop for over 30 years and it runs as true today as it did the day I got it. I've never needed to service this spindle, just adjusted the carriage screws right there as I'm working, add a bit of fine motor oil for lubrication and off I go with barely any loss of work time. This is a great spindle for any student who wants only one type that allows multiple, versatile uses from large to small work.

The other Babbitt style is a single directional shaft, scaled down in size that is very commonly employed in Idar in the cameo/intaglio studios. This smaller scale Babbitt spindle style I use exclusively for my intaglio/cameo style carving and precision style carvings. I use my hand shaped steel tools that I charge with different Diamond slurries that I mix in my studio for a heavier concentration of Diamond particles than the over the counter commercial pre-mixed Diamond compounds. With this spindle, I do not run water as a lubricant, but a fine light clear mineral style oil for lubrication and flushing of the gemstone as it is ground away.

All three spindles have between several inches to over a foot reach from the arbor house to the actual fine Diamond tip. The huge advantage over this versus the rotary style flex shaft is that I can literally carve very deeply into a cavity of the stone with absolutely no worry of the end of the shaft bumping up against the stone. I have carved chalices and bowls with a depth of eight inches and have not had a single issue. The other major advantage I've mentioned above is I can hold the gemstone with both hands, bring it up to the carving tool and have maximum control and versatility while carving. This same style of carving with a similar spindle is also used in the glass crystal style of etched glass design in stem wear and bowls.

Included with the basic spindle, one needs a huge assortment of various sintered Diamond tools that can run in the hundreds if not thousands of dollars per tool. So, I calculate to start a basic professional carving studio one needs to minimally invest around US$10,000 - $12,000. Of course, a new student or hobbyist can invest a lot less to get started. I feel to create the type of work and speed in which to create my pieces as a professional one needs to invest thousands in spindles, Diamond tools, faceting laps of assorted mesh Diamond powders. One is only limited by one's tools and of course one's imagination.

One of the most critical and almost essential elements in creating unique one-of-a-kind gem carvings is you have to build and maintain an enormous inventory of shape and type of carving tools. There are those sintered manufacturer tools and plated Diamond tools that come in a range of shapes and sizes but they don't always work for a particular curve or angle. So, I will reach for a piece of soft tool steel and like a lathe, I will shape the steel in the shape and size needed. This practice dates back hundreds of years, long before there were manufactured Diamond plated or sintered tools one could buy over the counter. Even today, this type of homemade tool is commonly used by cameo and intaglio carvers. You cannot really do the type of work I'm known for by just using over the counter diamond tools and products. The Gem Carver and even the glass engravers will shape steel or copper then charge it with an abrasive. Nowadays it's Diamond that is in a wide range of particle sizes depending on whether you require a coarse, medium sanding or a pre-polish surface. One applies the Diamond via a paste in the form of a slurry and with the simple pressure of the steel against the stone the diamond particle becomes embedded into the steel and you have a homemade, sintered-like Diamond tool. The huge advantage of being able to make your own tool is you can virtually create any size, angle or shape and not be limited to what is sold over the counter. Plus, commercially made Diamond-plated tools quickly wear out. Sintered Diamond tools become misshapen, whereas homemade steel tools can be reshaped as you're working, and by constantly applying more Diamond slurry to increase the grinding or sanding as you work on the stone. The huge advantage of the sintered Diamond tool is they can last for decades over the nickel-plated steel Diamond burs. Though the cost for sintered tools can be at least ten times the cost of plated steel Diamond burs, they do last for a very long time. I still have sintered Diamond tools I regularly use almost on a daily basis that I bought 30 years ago. I have no problem paying the huge difference in price up front because I know the tool will last me pretty much the lifetime of my career.

I make almost all of my own Diamond paste in my studio for several reasons. I can buy the Diamond powders at a more reasonable cost than over the counter slurries and paste, plus I can mix my own stronger concentration of Diamond to compound the ratio that one finds in the pre-mix offered. There is a huge advantage in that my work time is shortened because of the stronger Diamond concentration that gives me a more aggressive cut as I'm working the gemstone. I also use over the counter Petroleum jelly, but I've seen the Indians use room temperature coconut butter, beauty cream in China and other carvers use hydrogenated olive oil. The important fact is the slurry cream is thick at room temperature but melts as one carves away which generates heat, thus it turns to a liquid and flows the ground gemstone powder away from the stone and keeps the gemstone cool from cracking under the heat that is generated - except in Jaipur, India where the ambient high heat of the day keeps it in a liquid state. You need to have the slurry in a gel-like paste form in order for it to stick to the steel or copper wheel, then with the load of working the stone against the metal the Diamond particles imbed themselves into the custom-shaped tool. Basically, one is creating a homemade sintered style Diamond tool.

One keeps adding more Diamond slurry to the homemade shaped tool. The Diamond particles become embedded into the soft steel, wood, canvas, etc in the tool, but each material that the same size Diamond becomes embedded into leaves a completely different scratch pattern.

One of the things I would like to share about the actual act of carving a hard gem material, is that once one has negatively cut into the stone with a coarse Diamond tool, it can take five times that period to polish that negative space. Simply said, if it takes me one hour to carve something, it can then take me five hours to just sand it smooth and get a water clear polish. This is very different to when placing a flat surface such as a facet or convex dome like a cab where the sanding process can move to a much greater degree of efficiency, because you can cover a large area at one time with the sanding tool. When one goes concave into a hard gem material, the area of sanding becomes very limited by the tools one can use to sand, hence it can take five times longer to achieve the polish.

After one has carved with coarse to finer Diamond particles with a steel or copper tool then it's on to this several step process of sanding and polishing - depending on the mineral species. A quick understanding of the effect of the Diamond and the medium of your tool (such as steel, copper, woods, plastics or canvas, etc) can have on the surface of your gemstone. An example 600 mesh Diamond powder applied to a steel lap will carve and cut, but in canvas it is a fine sanding surfacing ready to be polished on Quartz. In other words: the harder the medium, such as steel, versus a soft canvas surface can leave a very different surface when one is using the same size Diamond particle. On steel, it will grind aggressively and on a soft, forgiving surface such as canvas surface, the same size Diamond particle will almost polish the stone. The hardness or softness of the medium has just as much to do with the grinding or sanding as the Diamond particle that is doing the cutting. An experienced Lapidarist knows which medium to use with which Diamond particle size to use in order to achieve the desired effect. In other words, different surfaces of the medium, such as soft steel, copper, wood, canvas or a factory made Diamond plated tool with the same Diamond particle will leave a very different scratched surface. For example, a soft steel 600 mesh is a grinding surface for Quartz where a canvas surface charge with 600 mesh is the pre-polish surface ready to be polished. Every medium has its own properties depending on how hard the medium is from steel down to canvas.

It takes years to understand the multiple approaches to the various tools and how each tool with the applied Diamond coarseness to fineness can have on each different gemstone species. Each gem species has its own hardness that responds differently to the same tool with the same diamond particle size.

Couple this with how every gemstone has its own refractive index, and the angle in which light bends as it enters the stone; the critical angle. One needs to know this critical angle, which means the shallowest angle one can cut the stone to the eye of incidence without the light bleeding out the pavilion and creating a windowed stone, thus ending up with a lack of brilliance and a dull looking stone.

Then once you have a full comprehension of the hardness of each gem, you have to then consider the cleavage of each species. This is the weakest atom bond in a given plane, where it is nearly impossible to achieve a polish because of the weak atom bond in that given direction it will continue to fragment and scratch the surface. Great examples of this are Kunzite, Csarite (Diaspore) and even Topaz. Even though Topaz registers eight in hardness, if you're right on the cleavage plane it's totally impossible to get a polish. So, one needs to know this and the given rule is to orientate the gem at least five degrees off this cleavage plane, ensuring that not one facet is parallel to the cleavage plane of that stone.

Most gemstones that are dichroic and trichroic give off very distinctive colors as viewed from different directions along the crystal axis. Other than gemstones that form in the Isometric crystal, such as Diamond, Garnet and Spinel, one must take extreme care. This degree of dichroism or trichroism can make or break a beautiful gemstone. A great example of this is Iolite, Andalusite or Tanzanite. Tanzanite has three very distinctive colors as it is viewed from different directions. In one direction one sees blue, another is purple and the third direction is a brownish red color. In the case of Tanzanite one heats the stone and thus can drive out the undesirable brownish red color. But then the cutter needs to orientate the gem just right to achieve the desired color. In the case of Tanzanite, the blue is the most favored color, but in the industry one sees more of the purple because due to the crystal habit shape one can achieve a greater weight than cutting to maximize the blue. Here is where one must diligently balance maximum weight retention to the most desired color. When working with an expensive gem material like Tanzanite this can be a real challenge.

People often think Sapphire and Ruby are hard to cut because they are the second hardest gemstone: nine on the Mohs scale next to Diamond which is 10. But to me this is not what makes Sapphire so difficult to cut. It is achieving the maximum weight retention due to the high value, whilst achieving the most desirable color. Couple this with Sapphire's tendency to be highly color zoned with areas of richer color in different parts of the crystal with almost colorless areas and this makes the stone a real challenge. So again, it is all about orientation. Placing these color zones just right in the cut of the stone, with the right direction because of dichroism can make or break the ultimate beauty of the stone thus affecting the end value of the stone, sometimes by many thousands of dollars.

These are just a few of the obstacles a Gem Cutter must learn and normally will take years to master. I can teach a student to cut a Quartz in a week, as it is very forgiving. The real mastery which can take upwards of eight years to learn, requires developing a thorough understanding of the uniqueness and approach to each and every mineral species with their corresponding properties of hardness, cleavage, crystal habit affecting light and color, to mention the obvious.

Other complications can be within the same species such as Tourmaline or Garnet from different localities from around the world. Some can react very differently depending on the geology that formed them. An example is Tourmaline, where the crystal structure can be so tight and there is extreme tension in the atomic bonding that the slightest degree of temperature while cutting, coupled with the speed of the wheel turning can literally have the stone explode on the dob stick. The water temperature used as a coolant must be just right, the lack of chatter in the grinding and the right speed one must know from different locations for the same species such a Tourmaline and some Rhodolite Garnet I've encountered in the world.

Some of the other unique aspects of being a Gem Carver is the tooling. So many of the tools one needs to create original works of art cannot be purchased on the open market. I still practice age old techniques of shaping my own soft steel bur shapes and then charging with a Diamond slurry of various roughness or fineness. This is the key to being able to create some of the most original and creative designs in gemstones.

Often I need to spend many hours shaping and making my own tools long before I can actually begin the carving process. Then once I have made a tool, let's say in steel, I need the same shaped tool in possibly copper and woods of different hardness, applying the proper Diamond grit of finer and finer micron size to begin the sanding process. This is also key in knowing that each species responds differently to the medium the Diamond is charged to. It takes years of trial and error to know if you should use, let's say, a very hard wood like ligma vita, birch, maple or even a certain type of oak to name just a few types of wood I use in my studio. Each wood has a different hardness and will leave a surface very different on let's say a Quartz versus Garnet or Tourmaline. Then, knowing exactly what steps are the best in applying different Diamond grits from 600 to 1200 onwards to 1800, 3000 all the way up to 50,000 Diamond mesh which is very fine. Then, where to stop with the Diamond on certain stones and apply a polish with rare earth oxides such as cerium or aluminum with certain species of gemstones.

As mentioned before, every gemstone has an ideal progression of steps, as well as medium of material to apply the Diamond to in order to achieve the ultimate, which is a water clear polish. I often say you don't have a gemstone until you have a polish. This is the hardest of skills. This is where one can see how many years of practice it can take to be a true Master of the art. The possibilities are infinite. Many of my complex Agate Chalcedony carvings take me hours and hours to achieve a water clear polish.

One can see how it can take years to master many of the variables to truly master all the various colored gemstones from around the world. So, you can just begin to comprehend how it can take decades to master the art. For me it was not till my 15th year when I really began to come into my art where skill merged with my imagination to dream up many of the complex styles I've created. Now after 40 years in the field I still feel my best is yet to come. It truly is a life-long pursuit. I am still learning new techniques and qualities about different gemstone species to this day.

8

BACK THEN A BREAK FROM TRADITION

· A Rare Self-Taught American Gem Artist in Idar-Oberstein, Germany

After 10 years of being self-taught, I longed to venture to this small village in Germany known as Idar-Oberstein, where there was a 500 year tradition of gem cutting and the birthplace of European Gem Art. It was the land of the Holy Grail for an aspiring Gem Artist working alone in America. There I had the rare opportunity to meet and eventually work with carvers whose families had a tradition of three to seven generations in the field. And I know for a fact the only reason I was allowed into these Gem Artist workshops was they could not believe I was self-taught, plus they were all impressed by my polish and how water-bright and clear it was.

I have been told by several reliable sources that I may have been one of the only Americans - if not the only one - allowed into a Master's working studio and to then work alongside them co-creating, who didn't have a formal apprenticeship training. Especially since I didn't even go to their Edelstein

(Gemstone) Lapidary School. The year was 1986: I had lived for 10 years in obscurity working alone, creating and honing my skill outside the box. The Master Craftsmen of Idar were extremely curious to know what I knew and how I had taught myself. This is what I believe got me into the door of one of the finest Holy Grails of Gem Art the world has ever known. For me, I wanted to know what had been a long and well-developed industry in Europe over all these centuries. Even today Idar is recognized as home to some of the finest gem cutting houses that adorn some of the famous major brands in jewelry and gem sculptured art.

In Germany, in order to become a lapidarist and hang your shingle and call yourself a Master, one has to go through a five to seven year program and apprenticeship alongside a Master. Up until this point, outsiders were never allowed to learn and work with these European Masters because it would have been almost impossible for a foreigner to even be let into their school back then. With the world economy now, in 2015, this is not so much the case, but back then I was the novelty and gossip of this very small village in the Hunsruck mountains of Central Western Germany, an hour and a half drive west of Frankfurt in the state of Rheinland-Pfalz.

The difference behind my self-taught path and the path of one who would go through the training in Europe, was that I had total freedom to work in the various techniques without any restrictions. This is in direct opposition to one who would enroll in the school in Idar-Oberstein. There in the beginning, one would be introduced to the many different techniques of cutting such as faceting, cabochon cutting, carving, cameo or intaglio engraving. Once the teachers recognized where the individual's skills were best placed, you would be placed on the path to spend the following years to master and train with that Master in the specific discipline. For me, growing up without boundaries I was able to explore whatever my heart desired. I started out only wanting to carve and sculpt in gemstones, then later moved on to faceting and engraving. This allowed me to explore the various techniques without a tradition telling me what I could and could not do. I was able to explore and invent techniques that I later discovered in Idar-Oberstein did not even exist. I was able to explore outside the box not even realizing I was creating new styles and techniques that had not ever been done before. I have come to realize this is why these German Masters were so willing to open their studios to a foreigner, one from the outside.

I believe because I had been inventing outside their box for 10 years prior, and had invented and created a whole new way of looking and working with gemstones, that in a small way I was about to change their world as much as they changed mine. Like Bucky Fuller said, I was to become one of those mavericks who was about to create a whole new model and make parts of these century long traditions obsolete.

Back in 1986, the journey with my wife Sharon to this small village with a very long history was exciting and pure magic. We pulled into this town without a clue or knowing a soul there. We were completely open to whatever came our way. For the first couple of hours we were driving around Idar looking for a place to land and find our way.

Idar-Oberstein is actually two small villages along the Nahe River that grew and eventually over time to such a point where there was no distinction between where Idar began and Oberstein ended. For centuries Idar was known for gem cutting and carving and Oberstein was known for the jewelry.

After about two hours of driving around between Idar and Oberstein, we spotted a small little Italian Restaurant. We decided to stop and eat and then decide what to do next. This is where all the magic happened. While enjoying our sumptuous meal of Italian food we ask Mario the owner; does he know a good place we can stay for the night. He immediately responds that directly across the street is a great bed and breakfast place owned by a local woman from Idar and her husband, who is an American.

As we pull up to the guest house that appeared more like a private home than a hotel, we gingerly knock on the door, still feeling a bit nervous and unsure this is the right place. As this attractive woman comes to the door, our first question is, "Do you speak English?". With absolute perfect enunciation and with only the slightest German accent she says, "Yes". Then we ask, "Is this your guest house and do you have rooms for rent?" Again, with much relief for Sharon and me, she responded with a warm and friendly, "Yes, and please do come in!" It turns out this is her family home she grew up in and now has opened her doors to travelers and visitors coming to this charming quaint little village that dates back over 500 years.

So now that we're here, what next? It's not like there are signs to the various Gem Carvers' studios or a tour book explaining where to go and who to see like one might find in famous wine countries. Still feeling a bit nervous and unsure as to how to go about experiencing Idar, we strike up a conversation with Claire about maybe we could start our tour? In our morning conversation over breakfast I share with her that I am an American Gem Carver and I've come to Idar to meet and visit some of the German Gem Artist studios. Luckily I had the smarts to bring along a few of my carvings and a highly polished Quartz crystal. When I pulled out my art she immediately showed interest and seemed very impressed that this unknown America, with no formal training, could have done the work that she was now looking at. Wow, it was the start of the most magical day. As my dream began to come true, she says she knew a carver here in town whom she thought I would like to meet. This day would be the beginning of experience and journey forward for the next 20 years I will never forget. The impact it would have on my life then and till this day has molded a huge piece of my career.

Claire is on the phone, calling up this Gem Carver and is speaking in German about an American whom she has as a guest in her inn and would they be willing to meet with me. She thinks I'd really enjoyed meeting one of Idar's older families that has been carving in the valley for three generations.

So, off Sharon and I go. There would have been no way we would have ever met this carver because in almost all cases they live and work out of their homes. There may be a small shingle sign hanging on the outside of the house but even this was not obvious to our eyes. To meet most of the carvers and cutters in Idar one really would need to be referred to by another in the valley.

It's a four storey home perched on a hill off the beaten path. It is just a home, with absolutely no way of knowing what is being created behind these walls from the outside. So we climb the stairs and knock on the door. Slowly the door opens just enough for a pair of eyes to peer through. We introduce ourselves as the Americans Claire called about. There stood a woman and a man. His English was very broken but his wife spoke fairly good English. Enough for us to begin a conversation. My German was zero, and in those days, I could not even understand a menu in a restaurant. I tell them I'm an America Gem Carver and have come to meet others like myself. I pull out my wares to show them, a wide grin crosses their faces and their door swings wide open. The next thing we know, we are being invited into their showroom. The carver is Bernard Becker, third generation, and along with his wife Renta they are of the tradition in Idar of what is termed in German "Plastik" Edelstein engraving.

Plastik is the type of carving that one does to form: birds, fish, animals, humans and plants of all sizes and shapes. From jewelry size pieces, up to very large sculptures and objects. It is the skill where one carves several different pieces of gem material – tongue and grooves – then these separate pieces interlock with one another and glued to form a whole sculpture. This style of carving was highly developed and refined during the Fabergé era. One can look back over a 120 years ago in the Gem Art books on Fabergé and see human miniature replicas of men smoking pipes, dressed in shirts, trousers, heavy jackets with folds in the fabric, hats on heads that are all composed of several different varieties of gemstone material. I later came to be told that many of Fabergé's works of art were carved in this very valley. And in all cases, if not most, credit was never given for the craftsmanship.

I'm totally enthralled and blown away by his work and art. Here in Bernard's showroom were huge eagles with wing spans over two to three feet in their spread done in clear rock Quartz crystal, Lapis and even cabochon grade Ruby. So amazingly real was his art, I must admit I was totally overwhelmed and blown away. All of a sudden I realized I had so much to learn, even after my 10 years working alone and in obscurity. My art up to this point paled in comparison.

They did ask to see my few samples. Somewhat embarrassed I pull out my pieces to share. The next thing I knew Bernard asked me, "How did you get such a high level of water clear polish on your pieces and especially in the large Quartz crystal?" Wow, he seemed very impressed to know that I was self-taught and that I could have come to achieve this level and degree of mastery without a teacher. I never did get to see his workshop that day, because like almost all studios in Idar back then the doors were closed to all outsiders. One generally only gets as far as the showrooms. But we exchanged contact information and promised to stay in touch.

From this point on the doors to some of Idar's finest began to open, one Master at a time. Bernard, as we're getting ready to leave says he knows someone whom I should meet and would really enjoy seeing my work. The dream is unfolding right in front of my eyes. He's on the phone to a friend who is world-renowned at that time for cutting some of the if not the largest gemstone spheres in the world. He name is Dieter Jerusalem and his showroom and factory are way out in the outskirts of Idar. Again, I would have never found his place without an introduction and direction if it was not for Bernard and his wife, Renta.

With directions in hand we are now traveling through thick forest and rolling green hills in the back country of Idar-Oberstein to a small hamlet called Herrstein. As we enter this huge showroom filled with gemstone spheres of all types of material and literally all sizes we meet his wife, Elisa. We are sharing our story with her and I pull out my few pieces once again. The next thing I know she says to us, "Wait here, my husband Dieter needs to see this". I am continuing to be blown away at every turn on my first day in Idar. He comes running out and with excitement. I find out that Dieter is the seventh generation gemstone cutter of his family. He even mentions that his family goes back as far as the Crusades in the 11th Century. Thus, the last name Jerusalem. Dieter appears to be impressed that he is meeting a completely novel and unique individual who is self-taught and has achieved this level completely on my own. I later have come to realize this was so outside the box for these Masters, since almost all of them spend years of study in their school and under the guidance of a Master.

How could this kid from America, without any formal training, achieve what I had accomplished on my own? He was also totally impressed by my water clear polish. I have come to see that my polish was much higher and scratch free from what almost all of them had been taught on how to get a polish on a stone. I came to realize I knew something they didn't and that they were extremely curious to know my secrets. I would come to learn that my self-taught discoveries in certain techniques, working outside the box, would be my greatest asset that allowed me to meet these Masters. They wanted to know what I knew and likewise, I was so curious to know what they knew and what type of equipment they used.

Upon the short but intense interchange, Dieter says there is someone I think you would like to meet. His name is Bernd Munsteiner. Are you kidding me? I knew of Munsteiner from a few years back during my gemology studies at GIA. He was the one back then who broke the mold of tradition and did completely novel and unique faceted and carved abstract gemstones in very rare transparent materials. He has been called the grandfather of fantasy cut gemstones. You might say he invented the concept and has inspired numerous others both in Idar and the USA in this form of technique with transparent gem material. At the time, he started this concept of cutting in the valley he was ridiculed and criticized for his new style of cutting. Ten years my senior and equipped with a complete training in lapidary skills, he ventured off to invent and create what would be a whole new style of cutting the world had never seen before. Here I was on my first day in Idar-Oberstein, going from one Master's workshop to another. It was so magical, like a dream, but in my full waking state. The climax of this first day in Idar was to meet someone I truly admired and looked up to in this art field. I could not have imagined that morning when I awoke that I would be standing in Bernd Munsteiner's studio showroom by the day's end. Stuff like this is almost fairy-tale like. A Master in Idar letting in a complete stranger, who had not gone through the rigorous training at the Fachschule Edelstein (Gemstone School) was completely unheard of in the valley of Idar in those days. Technically speaking, an individual, of Germany origin, in Idar had to go through the training in this school to then be able to work alongside a Master. It was completely unheard of in the valley of Idar in those days or ever before then to let a foreigner, who had not gone through this training.

Dieter tells me there will be no way I would be able to find his studio, so he graciously offers to have me follow his car as we drive further into the countryside to an even smaller village called Stripshausen way in the middle of nowhere. In this tiny village at the end of a road is Bernd Munsteiner's studio and showroom. His home lies 20 feet behind his studio/showroom.

I had a great time admiring his mastery and completely unique Gem Art. He is a living legend and here I am sitting down and having a conversation with him. He is, in my opinion, the one individual who has changed the course of gemstone fantasy style the world over. We have remained friends over the years, meeting at trade shows, speaking at the same conferences and sharing dinners together. He is now retired but his son Tom is carrying on the tradition of the family name.

This was my first day in Idar and I got to meet three very different types of lapidary Gem Artists. It would be a true highlight in my life, one I will never forget and that led to a door that would have never opened to me had I not come to Idar and met Claire in her guest house in Oberstein.

Upon our return from our European tour I received an invitation from Bernard Becker to come back to Idar and work in his studio. I could not believe this at first. Remember, on that first day in Idar no one was willing to take me into their workshop. That first trip I never got to see their equipment and observe them working. The doors were closed and I only got to meet each of them in their showrooms. He literally had to write me back again and tell me, "Yes, I would like for you to come back and spend time in my workshop." This was a golden opportunity I could not pass up.

The following year I made my way back to Idar and spent two weeks in his studio. There I got to see and work on their equipment, learn their tooling and many of their techniques. I have been told by several reliable sources from Idar and who know the valley tradition, that I was most likely the only foreigner at that time, certainly the only American ever to be allowed to work in the studio of a trained Master. Every year after that, I would return for two weeks and work alongside Bernard. I learned techniques that might have taken me years to figure out and master. I was now on the fast track in my training that continued for another five years. I was also introduced to their equipment and tools that I quickly bought and exported back to the US to employ in my studio. As our friendship grew, I returned year after year for two weeks at a time.

Based on my experience of perfecting the art of polishing very large crystal faces that are over one to two feet in length and Bernard's skill in carving in cameo and intaglio, I had a vision if I could carve by intaglio a scene or human face we could create together a complete brand new style of Gem Art the world had not seen before. We began to discuss how we could collaborate. See, when one looks into a finely faceted gemstone you see brilliance but can't understand how light bouncing around inside a well-faceted gemstone before it exits through the table. It is all so very abstract. But if you carve an image that the human mind can comprehend and bounce it around inside a gemstone, then one can marvel and enjoy the beauty of reflection and refraction. Thus, the birth of Visionary Gem Art was conceived and born. We would go on to create several different pieces along this concept.

The year was 1992. My reputation began to spread in the valley as this American with unique ideas and techniques who was working in Idar. In those years, I was completely novel and unique as an outsider that was spending time in studios working with known carvers from Idar. I was now being offered to come and spend time in their studios and play alongside these Masters. After six years of returning to the valley to work and study, I was at one of GIA's symposiums in Los Angeles where this very large and robust man comes running towards me shouting, "Mr. Lehrer! Mr. Lehrer!" I had no idea who this man was as he was calling my name out in the crowd, running towards me. It was none other than the famous Erwin Pauly, a living legend in the art of cameo engraving.

I had come to learn the post-World War II history of Idar's recovery from the ashes of war, and how it was devastated during the invasion of the allied forces that ended the war. There was very little left of the valley with respect to carvers and gem cutting. Many were Jews either sent off to the concentration camps to die there or sent to labor camps to be the carvers of war medals for Hitler's army. There was little to almost no business in the valley after the war.

The one man being credited with bringing back the century-old tradition of cameo carving was Richard Hahn, a true Master of cameo and intaglio. The art in this tradition is owed to this one man for resurrecting the craft. Erwin Pauly was one of his brightest and best student in those days. Erwin has been credited for carving outside the box when it came to cameos. Up to this point, cameo engraving was either carving the Greek or Roman classics or for portraits of individuals. Erwin invented the style of doing very modern, Art Deco and very stylish in style cameo. He is pure genius and a revolutionary in the field for his day. He was also one of the very first to sign his work, considered blasphemy in the world of lapidary art. He is a free thinker and has had a major impact on the style of cameo and intaglio carving. Well into a normal age of retirement he is still carving to this day.

Back to 1992. Erwin is standing in front of me, inviting me to come and work and play in his studio. So, upon my next trip back in 1993 I could not pass up this opportunity. Though it was just for a day, his work and his spirit as an artist had an incredible impact on my art. We have remained friends all these years and as a matter of fact I was just with him recently, in 2015, at his granddaughter's wedding.

Now the plot thickens. The year is 1995. As Sharon and I are driving to Tucson to do our annual trade show, she asks me, "What would you wildest dream to come true be?" My answer was, to co-create with the Pauly family.

That year I was walking past a booth at the Tucson Gem and Mineral show and was stopped dead in my tracks as I look down in the show case and see the most amazing carved cameo. I was so blown away by the detail. I was looking at a cameo that had been carved of an elephant, with every wrinkle visible on the skin, intricately engraved in the Agate cameo. I look up to see the name of the booth and it is none other than Hans Ulrich Pauly, son of Erwin. I strike up a conversation with his wife Gaby by telling her I knew Uli's (his nickname we all call him) father Erwin. I am so impressed with this carving I have to meet Uli.

Later that day Uli comes by my booth in Tucson to introduce himself. He had heard about me from his father, Erwin. Uli and I are the same age and of the same generation. We immediately had this cosmic connection with very similar beliefs and spiritual perspective on life. We each knew we needed to get together and spend more time talking with one another. It was one of those connections where upon meeting for the first time, you just know them immediately and they seem like you've know them your whole life. Gaby, his wife, was scheduled to fly home the very next morning to Germany, but decides to cancel her flight and reschedules, feeling the same way as Sharon and I that this encounter was meant to be.

The next day during our breakfast that morning, we all felt this immediate bond of friendship and familiarity. We knew that Uli and I needed to work together and co-create a series of objects in gemstone sculptures. That morning we decide that Gaby and Uli are to fly to my studio in California in March the next month of that year, where we can begin the work on ideas we inspired to create. The four of us bonded and have remained very close friends for years now.

This encounter began years together of co-creation where we developed and created several large Visionary Gem Art sculptures, along the same lines of what I started with Bernard Becker years earlier. Uli and I were creating together as one. Two artists with the same philosophy, inspired to share a vision in stone. Each sculpture would tell a story, a story of one's personal path of spirituality and inspiration. From the bond of the four of us, grew several Gem Art pieces. It was a team where the wives were as much involved as Uli and I were in the actual work. I would travel to his studio in Idar and he would come to mine in California as these fantastic pieces would unfold. We were once again breaking a mold and creating works of art; an American and a German. Prior to this is was not even possible for two carvers from two different countries to work and create together.

The work was so well received it graced the front cover of Lapidary Journal Magazine; was on display at the Heritage Museum in Saint Petersburg, Russia; the Harry Oppenheimer Museum in Tel Aviv, Israel; and the Carnegie Museum in Pittsburgh to name but a few.

Here, Hans Ulrich Pauly shares, in his own words, an interview with Sharon Lehrer about what is has been like to co-create with Glenn Lehrer.

Hans Ulrich Pauly - Working With Glenn Lehrer

My first encounter with Glenn happened in Tucson in 1995; a cameo carving of an Elephant in shading technique displayed in our booth at the GLDA Show, drew his attention. We started talking, back and forth and we couldn't stop.

We immediately connected not only around business, but found we shared many other interests as well, including similar visions of the world. Together, with our wives, we explored the possibilities of how to co-create new forms of gem carvings that would express our common visionary ideas.

I enjoyed his openness and broad knowledge about crystals, from both the mineralogical and metaphysical perspective. I was taken by the possibilities of what a joint venture between our different backgrounds could open. My main experience was in traditional intaglio and cameo carving which I had studied with my father, Erwin Pauly. Glenn had more expertise in faceting and sculpting large and small gemstones. A cooperation sounded very exciting and seemed like an opportunity to learn and grow.

Back home in Idar, my wife, Gabriel, and I quickly agreed that we should "make hay while the sun shines," and a month after the Tucson Show, invested in a trip to San Francisco. The knowledge and ideas that Glenn and Sharon shared with us were inspiring and up-lifting. Coming from a very small town that had been cutting gems in the same way for 400 years, being with Sharon and Glenn was "wind under our wings".

Together we went through Glenn's extensive stock of optically clear and Citrine Quartz crystals and selected some exceptional rough for our first new creations. We were looking for specimens that would transport our vision into inspiring pieces of gemstone art. We explored different visionary themes, drew designs and drawings before we started to cut and carve. Glenn cut and faceted the stone to create the angles for maximum reflection of the internal and intaglio carving that I'd do.

It was fun to observe us play "ping pong," as each new idea would spark another idea. All had equal value and there was no competition between us. Having lived, trained and taught many carvers in Idar, this was a new experience which I thoroughly enjoyed. The freedom we gave each other was a wonderful gift that enhanced our co-creation.

Being in a new environment both physically and spiritually was a wonderful new experience. Glenn and I could work for hours on end in perfect symbiosis and a peaceful flow, often attentively observed by their cat, Mr. Friendly, who lay around my neck while I was carving.

Glenn's spiritual knowledge and his perfection of his cutting capabilities in large crystals, made him a treat to work with. Our back and forth way of working together was unique. We shared every aspect of each art sculpture, from deciding on the theme, modifying the first sketches and in the cutting process.

Our wives enjoyed each other and were intimately involved in the process, supporting us and our ideas in every way. Our creative and strong minded women were an intimate part of the overall synergy

The four of us became very close. We enjoy going on vacations and our children and their nephew and niece have spent many good times together at each other's family home. We are an extended family - Glenn's nephew calls my wife his German mom.

I am not shy to say, we - Glenn, Sharon, Gaby and I - worked at the edge of a new millennium in gemstone cutting. Our collaboration produced crystal carving, creating a holographic expression of intaglio cut figures that are reflected in and through the facets of the stones. The Sun Temple is a stunning example of this holographic effect. This new form was a major breakthrough from the old tradition of crystal carving, resulting in new wonders of beauty that no-one had ever seen before. Creating "Visionary Gem Art Object" with Glenn is a landmark in my own work together, as well as for the industry.

We have meanwhile ripened like good, rich grapes on an old vine stock and now are looking for new projects in wearable art using our long experience and fresh ideas to create more beauty in the world, and inspire visions of what is possible.

This next entry is written by Gabrielle Pauly, Hans Ulrich Pauly's wife about our co-creation of our Visionary Gem Art and our collaborative work together.

VISIONARY GEMART™ - Glenn Lehrer & Hans Ulrich Pauly

"Truly art and science meet in a very profound manner in each of these artistic creations by Lehrer and Pauly."
"Idar Meets California," by Si & Ann Frazier, Lapidary Journal, February, 1996

A new generation of Gem Art has been born through the co-creative team work of Glenn Lehrer and Hans Ulrich Pauly. Their transoceanic partnership is a combination of the best of the European traditions and the innovative multi-talented American spirit.

Hans Ulrich Pauly, a gemstone and cameo artist with the wide-ranging traditional apprenticeship of an Idar-Oberstein education, is internationally recognized as a consummate Master. Glenn Lehrer, a graduate of the Gemological Institute of America (GIA), has an excellent reputation as an all-around master of the lapidary and jewelry arts.

The artists start with a very large, optically flawless gemstone material which ranges from six to 15 inches in height. They create a holographic effect by engraving a naturalistic image on a specific face in the gemstone which has been precisely faceted for its optimal internal reflections. Your mind is immediately captured and taken into the crystal as you wonder at the mystery of the images appearing and disappearing while turning the stone. The intaglio carving is reflected many times, making you question which image is real. You actually have to touch and turn the crystal in order to distinguish the real from the surreal. Each piece sits on a sculpted base made from marble or metal.

Breaking free of the old tradition of working individually as Gem Artists, Lehrer and Pauly enhance each other's creativity, releasing a new form of art which neither could have achieved alone. Enjoy the results of their collaboration. You'll be surprised and inspired by the beauty and depth of their VISIONARY GEMART™!

What was incredible is normally one dreams and then creates in solitude. It is very uncommon for two esteemed artists in our field to come together and co-dream and co-create. Here, similar to my relationship with Lawrence Stoller, Uli and I were continuing along the same process of co-creating as two artist working as one. I had learned over the years with Lawrence this very process; two very strong and creative individuals come together in a single work of art. We were creating as one, yet each had invaluable experience and knowledge to contribute. What is required for the success of this type of endeavor is supreme trust in one another and a strong lasting bond of friendship. You might give an analogy likened to atoms coming together in attraction, bonding by electro-magnetic energy and forming a perfect symmetrical crystal. Where one left off the other would begin. Back and forth 'till these pieces were completed. Truly a synergistic process where the whole is greater than the individual parts. There has to be complete trust and respect for one another's abilities, to work alongside one another, enabling each individual to contribute their genius and integrate it into one single vision. Like Lawrence and I, Uli and I would never move forward with a sculpture until we both agreed this was the next step in the process.

Reconnecting with Uli's father Erwin at a family wedding in 2015, where he endearingly calls me by the name, "Glenny", the love and deep respect has remained enduring over all these years. It is rare to find individuals whom you can trust with your life, love through thick and thin, and co-create in art and business. A map in this world where intolerance seems to be on the rise and shutting one's country's boundaries are the cry to protect what one is trying to hold on to. In history, this has never proven to work. Those cultures that excel in genius are those that allow outsiders in, tolerate them and integrate the diverse ideas. All one needs to compare are the golden years in Ancient Athens, the Renaissance of Florence, Vienna of the late 1800s and early 1900s, and now of course Silicon Valley in my own backyard in the greater San Francisco Bay Area, to name but just a few. Each of these cultures opened their borders to allow new ideas and cultures to interchange and create together. Those cultures that lacked tolerance for religious or political views have died and vanished. History has marked this truth over and over again.

I feel so blessed to have developed lasting and loving relationships like this in my career. A testament to one's ability to trust, be tolerant of others and remain open to new ideas to relationships and life. My life has been changed in each and every one of these cross cultural and co-creative processes. I would not be the person I am today without having allowed, explored and experienced such diverse experiences, various cultures whereby my art and life have evolved beyond my wildest dreams. I know as a fact my art is a greater reflection to this fact.

I can't tell you how many times I hear from others who I encounter who say, "Wow you're living such an amazing life. Or, you are so lucky to work and do what you love".

I say to all: live life grand, be willing to step outside one's box of beliefs and attitudes and be open to change and new ideas. Make every day count and never take anything for granted. Be more than willing to fail and make mistakes, sometimes over and over again. Be gracious and grateful to others and all good will come one's way. I know this to be my truth. I am living the life I've dreamt for myself and my art is the outpouring of this very essence. Beauty begets Beauty (Lazaris). Which means to me if one creates and surrounds oneself in beauty, more beauty keeps coming in to one's life. Thus, "Beauty begets Beauty".

9

BAHIA AND THE REAL HISTORY OF MEGAGEMS

· The Mega Co-Creation of Two Gem Artists

"Bahia, the world's largest
transparent gemstone pendant."
Quoted from the **Gemological Institute of America** (GIA)

To be fortunate enough to cut one of the largest, finest, rarest gemstones on the planet in my lifetime as a Gem Artist is something I will always be grateful for.

Bahia is an optical clear Rutile Quartz sculpture that weighs over 450lbs and is suspended from two 3/16" steel cables like a giant hanging pendant. Bahia is now on permanent display at the Gemological Institute of America's International world campus in Carlsbad, California, USA. How I was fortunate enough to be able to cut and carve this magnificent giant gemstone, along with how it came to finally hang in the lobby of the recognized school and museum is the story I am about to tell.

Back in 1983 my good friend and co-creative colleague, Lawrence Stoller, came to me asking if I would teach him how to cut a crystal. You might say at the time he was my very first apprentice, though I was still learning and honing this craft on my own at that time. Within a short period we would become co-artists on an adventure neither of us could have done on our own at the time. Together we created something completely unique and original within the gem and mineral world. As a co-partnership we created completely outside the box for the times. A legacy was born when we came together to create as one. Lawrence was visiting a dealer we often got our Quartz rough from and noticed this very large piece of optical Quartz being used as a door stop. Asking the dealer about the piece, his response was that no one knew what to do with it. It was an internally near flawless 62lb piece of Quartz with a matrix of clay earth on the surface hiding the clarity that lay within this stone. Up to this point, large clear Quartz pieces like this would be cut down into optical sphere crystal balls or the classic four sided obelisks like those found in Egypt and the Washington monument. This was all that anyone knew what to do with these very large clear Quartz pieces.

Lawrence came back to tell me about this piece and that we had to do something with it. I had already been cutting stones for the last seven years and one thing I knew was that the larger the flat surface was on any gemstone, the exponentially harder it was to get an optical flat polish. Neither of us had any experience in faceting such a large piece. It was outside the box for both of us. Lawrence, being new at the time to gem cutting, out of his naiveté convinced me we should do this piece. Being somewhat experienced, my logic told me it could not be done. So much for thinking outside the box.

Lawrence's persistence kept insisting we should try. This is where the apprenticeship ended and we became co-artist and cutter, inventing a whole new field in large gemstone cutting around these mammoth Quartz crystals.

Eventually I agreed to go along and figured we could eventually work out how to cut and polish the stone. We would eventually invent the techniques that would be recognized as MegaGems and started the revolution of large clear Quartz standing generators that can now be seen in every metaphysical crystal stores around the world. The term "generator" is used in metaphysical circles to represent a Quartz crystal with a defined termination tip on one or both ends that is used in meditation and healing purposes.

Our very first completed MegaGems project would become known as the "Empress of Lemuria", circa 1986. The Empress of Lemuria became the master model from which all other large Quartz crystals were modeled. The Empress is the first of its kind in history. In its completed state, it weighs 42lbs. It would go on to be exhibited in Moscow in the Furstman Institute of Academy of Science. Lawrence and I worked in obscurity, constantly pushing the boundaries of a box that did not exist. It was exciting times and we both could feel the exhilaration and knowledge we were birthing something totally new and imaginative.

It would give rise to a whole new generation of natural Quartz crystal that would be cut and polished with the respect of the angles and shape of the crystal's natural habit of Quartz. Thus, preserving these ancient sentinels on our planet to be respected for what they are and held instead of being cut up into beads, sculptures or small jewelry gemstones. Of course, these have their place but up to this point no one gave much respect to these giants of gemstones. Cutting them with total respect for the crystallography, large size and clarity would generate a whole new respect and love for the ancient earth giants, much in the same way we as humans need to save and preserve the giant redwood trees from my state of California.

After the Empress we continued down this path and cut the second large piece known as "Ki", a 98lb. clear optical Quartz crystal, in 1987. Each time a new even larger crystal showed up at our door we refined the tools and techniques. Each time we worked on these large pieces we refined and developed our own tools, equipment and techniques to polish larger and larger flat optical surfaces. One of the laws of physics regarding polishing an optical surface is that the larger the flat surface the longer exponentially it takes to get a polish. In other words, let's say a 5mm face on a Quartz takes 30 minutes to get a water clear polish, then a 10mm surface could take three to four times longer, not just double. So, you can begin to imagine when Lawrence and I started to work on flat gemstone faces that could be as long as 1.2 meters (40 to 50 inches in length), it could take days to get a water clear polish on just that one crystal face.

As already mentioned, when I eventually went to Idar-Oberstein on my first visit I saw that our techniques of water clear and bright polished out shined anything that had been done ever in the 500 years of the historic village known for cutting the finest gemstones and sculptures. It was then I knew that working outside the box of conformity allows one to explore and experiment without being controlled or influenced by the tradition. I am grateful to this day that I was born and raised where this art was literally unknown. This has been a driving force to this day, to be able to create with total freedom and without restrictions. If they say it can't be done, then I'm even more motivated to do the impossible. I believe this is one of the main factors that created the opportunity for the doors to some of these Idar Masters to be opened up to me back in 1986.

So, by 1988 we had cut several large gemstones of different variety and species. At about this time, three of the largest finest Rutile Quartz crystals were being unearthed in Brazil. Rumor had it they were the three largest finest, optical Quartz crystals to be discovered in Brazil in the last 150 years. One weighed 1800lbs, the second weighed 800lbs. (that would eventually become Bahia) and the third weighed 500lbs. Stones of this size are extremely rare and I have been told that crystals of this size and clarity are discovered only once in a century or so.

From Frozen Light The Following Extract Courtesy of 'Circles of Light' by Lawrence Stoller, Co-Artist of the Bahia, on the Subject of Working Together

In 1983, Glenn and I embarked on an adventure together, exploring the mystical qualities of crystals and the arcane process of cutting and shaping them. The culmination of our 10 year journey was the creation of the MegaGems sculpture Bahia.

Glenn and I frequented the same circle of friends. I knew him as a talented gem cutter, but had no interest in stones or jewelry myself until one day when I saw Glenn wearing a crystal pendant he had fashioned. It so captivated me that I told him, "You have to show me how you did that." Fortunately, he was gracious enough to accommodate my demand. Glenn and I spent the next seven years almost inseparable, figuring out through trial and error the tools and techniques that would allow us to cut larger and larger crystals. Our obsession powered us through the difficulties and challenges of uncharted territory. We were the Lewis and Clark of crystal cutting, mapping a frontier of the great Unknown. And like most explorers, we had to learn to survive while we figured out where we were going.

We were passionate and doggedly determined to succeed. Had we been smarter, we might have gotten day jobs to support our families. But we were just naïve enough to plow into our shared passion, taking on each new challenge that presented itself with a "we can figure this out" attitude. Bahia was the culminating project that not only extended us artistically, but was formative in shaping whom we were each to become.

The grinding that Glenn and I did over the years was not simply for the crystals we fashioned. The intense process of working together to pioneer a new art form forced us to continually shed the skins of our "lesser" selves to grow into new people. We had no choice; it was either work through our problems or never see one another again. With the help of our loving wives, Sharon and Sunni, we continually chose the less comfortable path of working it out. The result of our willingness to evolve our friendship and place it ahead of hardships was ultimately rewarded by the creation of Bahia. Bahia was birthed from our commitment to maintain the integrity of our friendship, knowing if we did this, we could work through any other problems physical matter might throw *at us—such as sculpting a spectacular 800lb rutilated crystal. We were joined in our efforts by the brilliant efforts of metal sculptor Pepe Ozán.*

When admiring a work of art, the observer sees only the art. But beyond the curves and facets, the artist sees reflections, the agonies and joys comprising the process that changes one's life forever.

For Glenn and me, Bahia was this kind of art.

Like so many things in life, one's path takes you in directions you can't always fully understand at the time you're traveling them. But in the future, it all seems to make sense and the skills come together in a synergy that allows one to lift to new heights in one's life. At this time, Lawrence and I were receiving recognition for being able to sculpt these large rare pieces, through a relationship Lawrence had developed with a Brazilian whose family was one of the largest optical Quartz mineral dealers that sold then high grade Quartz to the electronic industry, and the owners came to us to cut their stones. They offered us a partnership with them to cut and sell what would eventually become known as Bahia. History was in the making. Just when the two of us had perfected the skill in cutting such large gemstones, Mother Nature would reveal and expose these extremely rare wonders of nature at this same time. To this, I always reflect on this historical synchronicity. Two kids who grew up in California with no family history in gemstones, practicing and honing the art of large gemstone cutting paralleled at the same moment that Mother Nature would reveal and expose one of the finest Rutilated optical Quartz crystals ever in history. Call it fortune, call it magic… it all came together in the year of 1989.

The Story of Bahia

This is the journey and story of how this magnificent large rare crystal was first discovered, then later carved by Lawrence and me. This is Bahia's story of how she would be transformed into the world's largest finest optical hanging gemstone that now adorns the entrance to the Gemological Institute of America's campus in Carlsbad California, for humanity to admire and be inspired by for generations to come.

As the story has it, it was 1987 and farmers in the state of Bahia, Brazil were clear cutting the forest in order to farm, raise cattle and grow coffee. What they would do is gather up all the fallen trees and brush in a large pile and light a fire to burn and clear the land. It was during one of these nights that the farmers noticed a bright shining light off in the distance reflecting the fire. The farmers knew what this could be in Brazil, recognized for its rare mineral wealth. So, in the morning they got up and went over to where they saw this shining reflection in the forest. To their amazement a small peak of the termination from one of these crystals was sticking just above the surface.   Stopping all work on clear cutting they began to unearth this crystal. It took over two weeks to dig around it, only to discover that there were three very large crystals together. The largest weighed 1800lbs, another weighed 500lbs, and what came to be known as Bahia weighed 800lbs, in the rough.

When word got out about these extremely large and clear pieces, a family in Brazil who deals in this type of material was notified and offered to purchase the three stones. The discovered location was literally miles from any paved or dirt road. To get to this location was not easy. First, one had to fly by small airplane, then ride by horseback to travel to this remote area to inspect the stone. In order to get these stones out, the farmers needed to roll it out using log wheels from the forest for miles to the nearest road where it could be then transported to the city.

Since Lawrence and I by this time had built a reputation for carving such large pieces, the son of this Quartz dealer whom Lawrence knew came to us and offered a partnership with us. We could choose which of the two larger pieces we wanted to work on. We decided on the 800lb piece because it was optical from top to bottom and double terminated, plus half of the material of the 1800lb rough was included. When one buys a rough stone and half is milky or included one needs to calculate the weight loss so one has a clear picture how much of the rough is actually cuttable. This can affect the price of the rough. The large 1800lb piece was eventually sold to my fellow and good friend, Gem Artist Bernd Munsteiner, who would cut the stone that would become known as Metaphorisis, a 212lb sculpture, along with several smaller sculptures from the cut off pieces.

Bahia was extremely rare in that it was optical from tip to double terminated tip. Lawrence and I were determined to cut it as one piece and retain as much of the original size and weight. When the stone was uncrated in California, you could not see its full clarity because a thick 1/2-inch layer of clay matrix was baked into the surface of the stone. After eight hours of sawing the first front cut to reveal the clarity, we could see two parallel cleavage plane cracks along the rhombohedral direction of the Quartz termination. But as the cleavages were just entering partly into the stone, not creating a major crack, we felt we could work around these flaws and integrate it into the design of the stone.

If one looks up in mineral books about cleavage in Quartz, almost every mineralogy book will tell you Quartz does not have a cleavage. The truth is every cutter who works in Quartz will tell you differently. It is not what is called a 'distinct cleavage' where in most cases one could physically hammer to separate the stone along its cleavage planes. A cleavage plane in minerals is where the molecules have the weakest electromagnetic bond, thus it tends to break in straight, even, flat planes when a physical or thermal shock is induced - like those pictures one thinks of when you see a Diamond cutter split the Diamond evenly by hammer. In Quartz it is what is called an 'indistinct cleavage' in that it is activated by thermal shock. This means if the stone is very warm and you lower the temperature too quickly it will crack along these perfect planes. And inversely if the stone is cold and you heat it up too fast it will crack along the cleavage plane as well.

After removing the clay surface from the large prism face of the crystal we could see two parallel cleavages along the rhombohedral plane of the Quartz. As we started grinding and sanding the large front face of the stone one could see the cleavage cracks creep along in the stone getting worse as we proceeded. Because so much heat was being generated on such a large gemstone, there was no way to control the cleavage from growing. This was such a major setback at the time. We were so focused on keeping it intact as one large gemstone that when the cleavage planes kept growing we were devastated. All of a sudden we could feel our dream of cutting such a large stone being dashed. I often compare the emotion as being like a death of a close loved one. You just have this most awful, sinking, painful feeling in your stomach. We just did not know what to do. For a time, it appeared we were going to end up with three separate, smaller, less significant gem sculptures. Having already spent several months and hundreds of hours working on our revolutionary masterpiece, we were looking at three stones instead of one. We were so upset at the time that we had to take a step back from the piece for over six months. We felt that we no longer had this great, very large piece of gemstone.

This time away from the stone turned out to be a blessing in disguise. It was during this time away from the actual work that Lawrence, his wife Sunni, along with myself and my wife Sharon would sit around and try and dream about what we should do. It was during this sabbatical that an "Ah-ha!" moment occurred. As we took a step back, we came to the conclusion that we now had to cut the stone into three sections but somehow remained determined to keep it as a single sculpture. This forced us to push the creative envelope out further and come up with a very imaginative solution.

It called on every bit of our imagination to think this through and step way outside of the box. Though Lawrence and I had done several large gemstones together, this was a new frontier for both of us. During our six month sabbatical Lawrence, myself, Sunni and Sharon sat around trying to come up with an alternative. It was during one of our brain storms that we came upon the brilliant idea to build a steel sculpture to bring the three pieces back together in a single sculpture. And then the ultimate goal to hang it from a ceiling was just the creative impetus we needed to get back on it. To create a single sculpture from this once single crystal and then hang it like a giant gemstone pendant was so outside the box of what we had ever done previously. It was just the brilliant concept that would re-invigorate Lawrence and me to re-commence the work and move forward. When we started Bahia, we initially thought it would take around 18 months. Ultimately, it ended up taking us five years in cutting, carving and polishing and then another two and a half years to work on the steel frame with the assistance of the late Pepe Ozán, along with the engineering to hang the sculpture from a ceiling.

After a totally of seven and a half years of ups and downs of cutting the stone and fabricating the steel frame, the story does not end here. Of course, our final goal was to sell the stone for the partnership group. This was easier said than done. Lawrence and I thought the world would just be running to our door wanting this rare, unique stone. We had our good friends and gemstone/mineralogy experts Si and Ann Frazier appraise the value of the stone. They had written several articles in the Lapidary Journal for me and Lawrence about various works of Gem Art we had done and had years of experience in the industry. They also spent years in Idar-Oberstein and knew other major gem works they could compare it to. The difficulty in placing a value on a stone like this is, nothing quite like this existed before. It was so outside the box to give it a fair value when there was nothing to compare it to at the time. They gave it a range in value from US$2 to 4 million in their evaluation.

With appraisal in hand, Lawrence and I then spent the next five years exhibiting it, transporting it back and forth across the United States for it to be seen and admired. We did everything we could for it to been seen and marveled at. We really wanted it to end up in a public place where individuals could come and see it and enjoy it for generations to come. We really did not want it to end up in some private collection where the world at large could not enjoy such a rare gemstone.

Towards the end of our long journey in cutting the stone and developing the frame to hang it, the late Vince Manson, head of strategic development for the Gemological Institute of America (GIA) heard about Bahia and came up to my studio in Northern California to see the stone. Vince was in charge of the building and development of their new campus in San Diego county and was dreaming of a magnificent piece like Bahia to be present in what he termed the Gem Tower. The Gem Tower is a tall 30-foot alcove in the entrance to the main campus building. This was exactly the type of piece Vince was dreaming to be on permanent display in this alcove. The tower faces exactly due east on the compass and has a long narrow window that went from the ground all the way up to the ceiling of this tower that lets morning light shine through.

It started out being shown at the new international campus of the Gemological Institute of America in Carlsbad, California. We were hoping the school would see its value and want it for their campus. After one year exhibiting it, the school was showing no real interest at the time in acquiring it, so we then transported Bahia across the US to the Carnegie Museum in Pittsburgh, PA. There it remained on exhibition for two years as a very popular exhibit. With still no real interest in anyone or any institution wanting to purchase it we then transported it back across the US to the Los Angeles County Museum of Natural History. There, Bahia was on exhibit for two years with still no interest in purchasing it. After seven and a half years of actually working on the stone plus five more just showing it, we were running out of options and ideas. Surely there was someone or place that could see the value in the stone.

Through my good friends, William Larson of Pala International and Edward Boehm from Rare Gem Sources, we developed a plan to return Bahia back to GIA for another exhibition, hoping this time the powers that be would see the value of having this stone in their museum collection permanently. Lawrence and I really felt that this was the ideal place for Bahia to be for generations to come to enjoy its rarity and beauty. More than just the money, we were hoping to realize after such a long time working on Bahia both he and I really wanted the public to be able to have access to enjoy and marvel at its rarity.

So, we moved Bahia from the LA County Natural History Museum back to the GIA, where it all started, and hung it for the second time in the Tower. Six months go by and still the Board of Governors could not commit to acquiring Bahia. Our Brazilian partners are now getting anxious for a sale. We all had a lot invested, both time and money, and by this point over 12 years had lapsed since we actually started cutting Bahia, including five years exhibiting it at three major US Museums. Still there seemed to be very little interest. We were then offered by a major US auction house to have Bahia be the cover piece of their catalog for the next major auction that they were having. This was a major breakthrough for us.

With only 48 hours to sign the contract, I call up Bill Boyajian, then the president of the GIA, who years earlier was my colored gemstone instructor. We remained friends and stayed in contact over the years. I told Bill about our predicament and that if the GIA was to do anything at this point they had 48 hours, otherwise we were going to take down the exhibition and move Bahia to the auction house.

Though my Bahia partners and I thought we could fiscally profit more by going through the auction house, by the time the house took its commission we would most likely end up with close to possibly the same amount of money in the end, and with no guarantee. With the GIA it was now a sure thing and it would remain public for generations to come and see it personally at the GIA. Lawrence and I just had to convince our Brazilian partners this was our best option and an almost sure thing to forgo the auction house and let the GIA run with the campaign.

I remember Bill saying over the phone to me, "Glenn, give me 24 hours to see if I can come up with a solution. We all love Bahia and would hate to lose the stone."

True to his word, Bill calls back in 24 hours and tells me he has an idea. He wants to run a campaign to, "Save Bahia" plus the GIA would be fulfilling the late Vince Manson's dream of having Bahia hang in the Tower which was what he always wanted. In a way it would be a memorial to the late Vince Manson's dream for the Tower. Never done before, the GIA developed a fundraising idea that individuals would donate to making Bahia a permanent installation at the GIA. Each one of the donors would have their names engraved in the wall as contributors to Saving Bahia. It was a brilliant idea and it worked.

Bahia by this time was so loved by the staff, instructors and students of the school that many of these individuals stepped up to contribute to saving Bahia. This was so impressive since many were on a tight salary as an instructor or staff member of the school. Because of Bill Boyajian's concept and ability to pull this off as the GIAs president/CEO, the campaign was a major success. Bahia now hangs permanently at the Gemological Institute of America world campus in Carlsbad California for generations to admire and appreciate.

One of the amazing caveats to this whole story is the Tower itself, with the window that faces due east. It seems as if it was almost intuitively placed there just waiting for Bahia to arrive. No one could have planned this one, but on the spring and fall equinoxes the sun rises in the due east direction and the light shines through this tall long window and directly into Bahia. As the light passes through Bahia the perfect example of refraction occurs on a grand scale. The light of the sun is refracted into the seven colors of the rainbow and shines down a very long, long corridor as the sun rises.

One spring equinox, I had to see this phenomenon myself. It is absolutely incredible that when the sun rises and as the light hits Bahia, a rainbow is cast on the ceiling of the entrance to the campus. Over the next half hour this rainbow moves down the corridor as the sun is rising, through big glass doors and ends up creating an amazing rainbow on the stair case that goes up to the executive offices of the campus. While I was there I witnessed several staff members of the GIA and students come to witness it as though it was this Stonehenge-like astronomical event. Truly a very special event to witness in person. Pure magic. Bahia is now there for others to see and enjoy this real miracle of nature.

10

THE STEVE AND GLENN STORY

· And All Things Gemporia TV

"Man is a genius when he is dreaming."
J.W. Marriott

What follows is a story of taking risk outside one's confines and the luck that comes with thinking outside the box to have an opportunity of a lifetime; a random chance encounter that has now become an amazing business relationship and deep friendship of trust and integrity. It is rare to find both in one's life, where you become good friends and have a unique business relationship with one person.

How did we meet? Allow me to backtrack to the fall of 2008, long before I met or even knew who Steve Bennett of The Genuine Gemstone Company was.

It was the beginning of the Great World Recession of 2008. Like many, I saw my business of 35 years literally lose 50%

of its income. In those three and a half decades, I had seen ups and downs in my business with a few months of really hard cash flow. But this was different than any other time in that it would continue for a year, then a second year. It was not local or even regional, it was worldwide. My stable income had been the mom and pop jewelry stores, the gem dealer, the jewelry designer, and my retail customers - all of whom almost disappeared overnight. We went from having weeks of work lined up in the studio to not one job, repair or order in our boxes. My steady gem and jewelry business of over 30 years was burning cash and drying up. It's hard to see something one has built so much of one's life into almost look like it would die. Hard to face and take a deep breath and make those hard decisions around something one put so much of one's life into. But I have never been one who would sit about getting depressed for very long. After a hard couple of years of managing the bleed out of cash and loss of business clientele, by 2010 I had to do something. So, my wife Sharon and I sat down and revisited our metaphysics. We were living our philosophy and doing our homework, processing and mapping out our change from where we were to where we wanted to be.

This is where putting function before form mattered when it comes to one's belief and attitude around living a spiritual and metaphysical life. It was a matter of how we wanted to be living and being in the world from this point forward, knowing what I knew and was capable of expressing. We sat down, listed all my talents and skills - not just my obvious artist abilities, but the skills and talents such as my acting and live public speaking along with some TV background - I'd even been on TV, live on the Oprah Winfrey show. (Please see chapter 13 for the full story.)

What transpired was how I wanted to live my life from a functioning state versus how I had done it in the past by just changing the form, thinking I could get it by achieving. For example, I clearly stated I only wanted to work with individuals I liked and who I felt held the same principles of trust and respect. No more chasing carrots with people who promised the moon but barely delivered on these big dreams. Up to this point I would compromise some of my own principles for the hopes these dreams would manifest. Most often the dreams would dry up or deliver half-baked results. I decided at this point in my life I would no longer compromise my principles for the sake of this dream if I did not like the person or felt it challenged my integrity.

From here, Sharon and I could see what areas of the business I could move forward and keep alive during this difficult time. From there we dreamt, visualized and did ritual for a virgin future where I could go on TV and sell my cut art gemstones and jewelry. It just seemed like the perfect medium and fit for my talents. Prior to this time, I had some start/stops with some of the largest television shopping channels in the USA over the years but nothing ever stuck or was not the right fit for me. But I kept visualizing this was one of those the perfect mediums I knew for me to sell my gemstones and jewelry designs. I just did not have a clue as to where or the means at this moment. But I knew if I only met the right person and understood the right combination of events this would be a big success. Call it persistence, but I remained focused and determined to make it happen.

Talk to any very successful individual and they will tell you they failed several times before that one opportunity became their big success. I persisted and failed several times up to this point but as already mentioned, I never stayed defeated for long. I was determined and more importantly I believed in myself that I had this destiny and a big piece of it was to create these beautiful, natural objects of wonder that would inspire others to feel creative and moved by beauty in the world. The message here is just keep focusing and with clear intent all good things come in time. This is such a powerful message in one's life. I've heard over and over again that one does not always get what one wants but one always gets what one needs.

As well as only wanting to work with individuals that held a similar level of integrity, genuineness and a long term commitment to making a partnership work, I also wanted to be able to create my gemstone jewelry designs in an affordable way so more individuals had access to these rare wonders without having to sacrifice my integrity. See, up to this point my work was very one of a kind and the cost to produce on a one-off level made so many of my works out of the range of affordability for most. It is fine to produce museum quality and collector level work, but it remained in reach to only the few that had the means to purchase my work. I wanted to be able to produce fine quality work that was affordable yet inspiring all in one piece. Sounds like a tall order but I was at this point still in the dream-visioning stage of this process, so there were no limits except what Sharon and I put on our vision work.

Fast forward to the April 2011 International Colored Gemstone Association (ICA) World Conference and Conclave that happens every two to three years somewhere in the world. I was asked to do work on the constitution/by-laws of the ICA since I had done the same for the American Gem Traders

Association (AGTA) while I was a board member. Because I helped work and complete the governing rules for the ICA organization, they gifted me free entrance to the conference. All I had to do was buy a plane ticket to get there. Even though I was still having financial difficulties, both Sharon and I decided it was just the right thing to do to jump start this new vision we had been dreaming of, to network internationally with associates I've known for years in the business. Besides the cost of the flight, with each conference they do a mine tour in the country. A couple of years back I was a speaker at the ICA conference in Australia and regretted that I did not go on the mine tour then. We both knew I needed to be on this tour. It was money I did not really have to spend, but once again we felt it was so important that we did not hesitate in spending the money because we felt it was just the right thing to do. Sometimes one needs to break free of the confines of one's life and take a major risk. You don't logically know why but the feeling was so strong in both Sharon and I that we did not even hesitate to consider the downside of spending money that was not there. Dreaming outside the box more often than not requires taking risk and giving one's current reality a slip. What I mean by this is even during adversity and lack you need to have courage to push beyond your boundaries to explore opportunities and challenges.

So, here I was in Brazil, first night of the congress standing around at the opening dinner. A mutual business associate introduces us. I did not know who Steve Bennett was or what his business was at the time. And I believe he did not know what I did nor who I was either. He graciously asked if I would sit with him and his family at their table on opening night. I learned that he runs a TV jewelry show in Great Britain. During dinner, we talk small talk and not much transpires during this time. Since he's with his wife, Sarah, his children and his father, they get up to leave earlier than most and we say good night.

After they have left I'm sitting there alone and happen to look down and notice a ring on the floor. I pick it up and figure it was one of his family member's pieces of jewelry. I put it in my pocket and figure I'll see him during the congress and ask if it's his to return. A day or so later during the conference I see Steve and ask him if this is his ring. This is where the smallest act can have the greatest impact. It turns out that it was his and the very fact I returned it to him had a major impact on him, that this person whom he did not really know would make an effort to return a ring that was found, that was his. At the time, I did not think this was such a big deal. For me it was just another ring and that I should find the owner and return it.

For me it all started when we were on a mine tour. It was a tour throughout Brazil to 10 different gemstone and gold mines. At the first mine in the state of Rio Grande de Sul I felt we connected. My nephew, Thomas Jeffrey, was helping me with my social media program that I was just beginning to start up. He gave me this small video camera and asked me to do some filming of the tour. I was down in this Amethyst geode mine off in a corner doing a selfie and talking about the geology, mineralogy and gemology. The next thing I realize is that there is a small crowd standing around listening to me describe the science of the formation of the Amethyst in this cave of rock. Steve, with his son Matt, were also down in the cave but they were there doing their thing with a major production camera for the documentaries they make for their TV shows.

Next thing I know, Steve asks me if I would be open to having him interview me about the geology of the Amethyst mine. For me, I'm always looking to share my passion and did not hesitate in the opportunity. This is where for me I felt we bonded. Going from mine to mine by bus there were usually several hours of travel time. Steve gets up in the front of the bus and walks back to ask if he could interview me for a book on gemstones he's writing for his customers. He wants to include a chapter on lapidary and by this time he had learned of my achievements and wanted to include me in his book. So, for about the next half hour as I tell my story of how I got into it cutting in the first place, and what some of my achievements were, he is listening intently but not taking any notes, which I find perplexing.

Once I've finished he gets up and walks back to the front of the bus. After about an hour or so he walks back to me in the back of the bus and gives me his iPad and asks me to read what he's written about me. He asks me to be sure he got the story right. As I read it I'm amazed how he has captured the entire story without missing anything of importance. With a wide grin, I say, "You got everything except for one main point." With a perplexed look, he asked, "What's that?". With humor I say, "I spell my name with two Ns, not one." Otherwise, without taking a single note while I'm sharing my story, I'm amazed how he captures my story with depth and detail. I'm thinking to myself, this guy is brilliant.

This was the beginning. As the journey continues he then proposes that I should come visit him in the UK and bring some of my couture pieces to go live on air to introduce his customers to my work and who I am as a Gem Artist. Then, after we've introduced my work and my story to his customers

I should go to Jaipur and work with one of his main vendors and try to produce my TorusRing cut in their factory so we can do a line of jewelry for Gems TV in the UK. He says there is only one of his vendors that he can think of that he thinks can do this level of cutting, his name is Manuj Goyal. With absolute astonishment, I tell him I know Manuj Goyal.

Three years earlier a mutual friend, Yianni Melas, world renowned gem explorer, introduced me to Manuj Goyal via a phone call believing Manuj and I should work together.

When Manuj and I were first introduced by Yianni Melas three years earlier, the timing was not right. Manuj's father had just passed away and it was just not the right time for him and I to connect. Though I did not know Manuj, he had known me from his days at the GIA as a student when I would come to the campus and give a talk to the students about Gem Art. He was one of those in the sea of eyes I would look out into as I shared my Gem Art and inspiration. I later discovered with Manuj that in his mind was this dream that someday he and I would work together. All things are full circle and here we were via our mutual friend, Steve, to be connected now and working with one another in his factory in Jaipur producing my gem cuts and jewelry designs at that affordable price Sharon and I dreamt was possible, we just did not know how until then.

Long before I met Steve, I had a dream whereby I could create my unique gemstone cuts in fine jewelry at affordable prices for a much larger audience. I did not know how, but I had a dream that my TorusRing cut was the perfect vehicle for being able to produce enough quantity to fulfill an audience as large as Steve's TV channel was offering. Through my chance encounter with Steve earlier that year in Brazil I was about to be able to fulfill this vision.

I was returning back to India after a 30-year sabbatical – a place which felt like my second home in the world, for sure from a spiritual place, to embark on a new odyssey where I would design and create my unique carved gemstone. No longer just creating my one of a kind gemstones and jewelry for the few who can afford it. Here is where the power to dream and envision one's true desire was once again a testimonial to living a spiritual life with integrity and driven by principle.

My style and techniques are completely novel and unique to a country that has over 500 years of gem cutting tradition. My style and concepts are something the Indian gem industry is completely unfamiliar with and has no idea how to create. One of the difficulties of working in a country like India is an issue of trust. Trust that your unique ideas don't bleed out of the workshop and end all over town being created by others. I had tried to manufacture my TorusRing cut earlier in China only to feel that the quality and integrity was lacking. I had to abandon my attempts in China for several reasons.

Upon meeting Manuj on my first visit I could feel this brotherhood of integrity and trust. We are now almost five years into our working together and the relationship keeps getting deeper and the quality of the work continues to improve and become a world class product. I stay with Manuj in his home as a family member, am close with his wife Kajal and play alongside his kids as an uncle. It is such a treat to come to India, live in his home and work alongside him and his wife Kajal creating magical jewelry. We have completed several very successful collections for Gemporia over the last five years for Steve and Sarah Bennett's TV channel, and the product is truly amazing and continues to get better and finer with each collection. I have fulfilled this dream where my standards of quality and beauty are able to be manufactured in Manuj's factory with outstanding beauty and magic. I not only have a very good business partner but a deep and lifelong friendship with Manuj. We are constantly exploring new avenues for my creativity and his genius to manufacture my work outside the box, with ideas I'm always coming up with.

Steve Bennett and I have also deepened and enriched our relationship as well. He is one of those rare individuals in business that means what he says and does what he means. He is one of those unique people I've met from around the world that truly only does what he deems fun. If it's not fun he's not interested in it. I truly believe this has been one of his winning successes as to why his business continue to thrive and grow.

As of July 2016, we have successfully sold well over 60,000 units worldwide, through Gemporia. We have introduced two brand new cuts called the QuasarCut and the KaleidosCut. We are always inventing new ideas and are constantly re-inventing my style. With Gemporia I am inventing, introducing new cuts and constantly coming up with new jewelry designs. Starting with the very successful TorusRing cut (see more about the TorusRing cut in the next chapter) and then the QuasarCut Collection, we've now moved into what has been called the Lehrer Bennett Collection. A collection of very fine top drawer gemstones such as Colombian Emeralds and Sapphires from around the world in my unique style of cutting that I personally hand produce in my studio workshop. We then set these rare single gemstones in fine 18k gold and platinum and offer them to his customers. And most recently I've introduced the KaleidosCut which is where another gemstone is placed on the underside of a QuasarCut. The effect is the second stone reflects in a star or flower pattern in the QuasarCut. A very magic and mysterious new cut.

Together we are constantly pushing the boundaries and always looking at new products to produce and introduce to his customer base on Gemporia. We are also now searching out unique gem rough from mines around the planet to bring to his devoted customer base, who have come to trust Steve fulfilling his pledge. A commitment, whereby he sources the gem rough from mine to market at incredible prices.

After observing and working alongside Steve over these past several years, I am always amazed that he never stops to rest on his laurels. Once he achieves what he has dreamt up, he is on to the next level, constantly pushing his success cube to greater and greater accomplishments and achievements. Let me explain what I mean by a "success cube" (Lazaris). Our levels of success are represented by the 3 parallel sides of a cube: height, length and depth. Think about standing inside a cube. The height is my ceiling of success. The width is how many areas in my life I am willing to succeed in. The depth is how deeply I allow myself to feel my success. We all have a level of success we are willing to allow ourselves to achieve whether I am aware of this or not. I can learn how to identify the levels of my success cube so I can choose to decide to expand my height, weight and depth of success.

Much in the same way I have all these years re-invented

myself, pushing past my failures to accomplish new heights, Steve is one of those rare individuals who is walking his talk. Always willing to change and adapt, I can see why he is so very successful in business and life. He is one of those larger than life individuals and at the same time a genuinely nice and approachable human. Even with his extraordinary success he is still a downright great guy. I have learned so much and have been truly changed in my life by our coming together in life. I could not measure the real positive impact he has had on my life. I would not be writing this book if it was not for him. He is one of those individuals that Sharon and I had programmed for a couple years earlier, whom I had dreamt I only wanted to work with. An individual one could trust like a brother and have nothing but fun working alongside. The amount of gratitude I have for our relationship is impossible to describe and measure. With Steve, I am now creating the destiny I have dreamt of for so many years.

11

FROM THE DREAM, TO THE FANTASIA, TO THEN GROUNDING IT ALL THROUGH THE EYE OF THE TORUSRING

· Forty Years of the Evolution of My Gem Art

"I am enough of an artist to draw freely upon my imagination. Imagination is more important than knowledge. Knowledge is limited. Imagination encircles the world."
Albert Einstein

From that first day back in 1976 to today I never did just the ordinary with gemstones. In those days, it was because of my naïvety to the actual art itself that I would be carving and dreaming up ideas that were unique and novel back then for gem cutting. Because I was flying solo for the first 10 years, I didn't have a soul to stand over me and instruct me what to do and what not to do. I was in a complete bubble, ignorant to the larger world of gems that had existed for centuries if not a few millennia. Not because the information was not out there, but because it did not cross my mind to even go look to research the topic. I was just dreaming and experimenting.

The good news is I could dream up anything in my mind's eye and then go about trying to figure how to do it. The bad news was, I paid for my education with all the mistakes I made along the way in the beginning years with countless hours invested and losses due to the destruction of a very valuable material that is my medium I create with. I have a graveyard of crack stones to remind me not to repeat that mistake again, if possible!

Those early years were not the most technically precise and lacked in quality but the creativity and concepts of how to play with light and refraction in gemstones grabbed hold of my dreams and spun them in so many wonderful ways of expression. From the first classic obelisk style, frosted clear Quartz crystal circa 1976 with the Diamond set in the center, to the Wings of Isis series of carved wings circa 1980, I felt I had found an endless well of ideas and concepts to explore the expression of my artistic mind and heart.

From the very beginning I was alchemically exploring and comprehending this new-found knowledge of the science of mineralogy and coupling it with the contextual emotional feeling of artistic expression. It was a melding of thoughts and feelings into one expressive form of beauty. I felt I was pursuing an ancient ritual in the craft of alchemy, instilling my spiritual heritage with each piece I created.

It is nature-based, much in the way my medium using

rare natural transparent gem material is transformed into something greater than Nature created herself. She took it to Her level of perfection by aligning elements to form molecules that then organize themselves in a 3D repeating pattern of geometry that creates something so transparent durable and clear. Then I come along, also a product of Nature, to innovate and take the knowledge of refraction to paint a prism of brilliant light and color. We think that to co-create is with another or a team of individuals. But another way we can co-create is with Nature Herself.

As a Gem Artist I feel and know I'm co-creating all the time. I'm considering the hardness, its angle of refraction, its durability with regards to how thick or thin I can carve it, constantly dancing with these natural properties as I wrap a dream into the creation.

The series of pictures (see photo sections) all bear witness to my efforts in the first nine years of exploration and self-apprenticeship.

The Birth of the Fantasia Series

The major break in my apprenticeship came when I started traveling yearly to Idar-Oberstein and working alongside Bernard Becker and then later with Uli Pauly. With Bernard my first piece was a carved red, green and brown Jasper that I carved as a grape leaf. Then on to a complex orchid two-piece flower in frosted Quartz that I then had Bernard carve a Hummingbird suckling from.

From this point on I was charging out the gate. I now had the tools and the means to carve any wild dream I could visualize. Due to lack of funds on my end, Chalcedony became my medium to venture and create with, due to the very reasonable cost and sheer diversity. Thus the Fantasia Series was born. I was inspired by the folds in the fabric that one would see in a Renaissance painting to the blurred images of Monet's Impressionism.

I would see images the way several people would see a cloud. From each individual viewpoint one would see a leaf, the fluttering of a butterfly wing or an angelic being in flight in the same carving. I would allow myself to see more than one image and fold them into one seamless carving. Each piece was a one off, left to the viewer's imagination in each gemstone. This was unique in that from the perspective of art for art's sake itself, an artist generally creates a whole image to stand alone and be a full expression of a vision or statement. I was creating art that I felt was only half done, but on purpose with regard to design. In other words, I would create just some of the expression, leaving lots to the imagination of a jewelry designer or goldsmith to come along and complete the inspiration. Each jeweler would see something completely different. In the next chapter is where I share the art of seven individually unique jewelry designers' use of my gemstones.

The Fantasia Series is the foundation where recognition as a Gem Artist came of age. I was beginning to win gem cutting awards in the US and abroad. So unique was my use of Chalcedony and Agate that I was beginning to be featured regularly on national and international trade magazine covers. This was the launching as a professional Gem Artist and an all-round lapidarist. To this day I still create this style, even though they are time consuming and most are one of a kind. The good news is each piece is a stand-alone original, unique in material and style. The downside is, our industry is based on numbers of reproduction one can do with the same size gemstone in a multi produced precious metal setting. Thus producing hundreds if not thousands of the same look. This is not possible to create with the Fantasia. Each is literally a one-of-a-kind. Though I love the style and inspiration of the Fantasia Series I would hit resistance from jewelry designers since it was not easy to reproduce more than one of each piece. For years jewelers would come by my booth in the Tucson Gem Show and say, "Glenn, I just love your gem carvings, but I need to create a mounting in gold each time". Hearing this over and over again in my mind, I started thinking how I could create a unique, one of a kind look that is also calibrated and reproducible. Thus, the Birth of the TorusRing.

The Genesis and the Invention of the TorusRing Cut Circa 1997

The story goes back to my early childhood. Ever since I was around five years old I could close my eyes and see the large green circle with a black center and purple on the edge around the green ring. As children do, thinking everyone could see this image I would play with my eyes closed moving it up, down, right to left and in circles. Thinking this was pretty cool. In science, it is called the Torus, or Toroid shape in nature.

I came to know what this image was later in my late teens and mid-20s from my mystical experiences on one end and my education in the science of mineralogy. It is the most prevalent form in which our known universe forms into. From the deepest of space involving quasars, spiraling nebula and planetary solar systems to the very micro world of atom with the field of electrons and protons. Circles inside of circles, like waves on the beach, hurricanes and tornadoes borne of wind and water. Just venture into your garden and you will see almost every flower there is a TorusRing. Look further and it is the rings on a tree, the unfurling of a fern fawn to many sea creature's shells. Nature can be so factual and circling and spiraling everywhere one looks. Just look into the eyes of us humans and there is the TorusRing as the window to the Soul.

Fast forward. Around 1982 I kept dreaming about setting a gemstone inside of a gemstone. I was infatuated with this concept. It started out with carving an internal hollow ball inside a gemstone and then mechanically setting the metal in the bubble then setting the gemstone inside the gold that was set in the larger stone. This worked but had very obvious flaws in the design idea.

First, when you drill and hollow out a bubble in a traditional faceted gemstone, you've also interrupted the path of light in this reflective space, so that all you then see is this bubble and loss of brilliance. The second downside is you have to set the gold into the outside stone first by reverse rivet into the bubble space, then attempt to hammer set the center stone into the gold that is set in this outer stone. Need I say more, other than that causing damage was always possible around the attempt to hammer set a gemstone into the gold setting, that is already being held by a crystalline gemstone body.

But not giving up on the idea of achieving a gemstone inside a gemstone my innovation marched on in other trials and errors. Then along comes a chance over a decade later in 1996. A goldsmith by the name of John Langenfeld came to me with an idea for a design he was working on for the AGTA Spectrum jewelry design contest. It was not related to what I had be attempting to do with setting a stone inside of a stone. He had designed a concept where he wanted me to carve pieces of a circle in Amethyst to border his inner aspect of the jewelry design he had in mind. I knew Amethyst would seem dull in a curved tube because there is not enough mass to hold a strong Amethyst color, it would be more of a pale violet almost like a Rose de France color. As he and I were discussing how to give this a richer color and more life I suggested we do a pavilion on the curve. So, imagine a long baguette style cut gemstone, but instead of it being rectangular and straight I would carve it with a circular curve. As I was creating this piece for John, I had the "Eureka!" moment. If I continued the curve into a complete circle and closed the ends I would have this perfect reflection with the classic inner cone and the hole in the center.

The TorusRing was born. It answered every shortcoming of my early attempts. The hole in the center with the internal cone maintained the perfect reflection without the hole being visible in the reflections. Actually, with the curved cone, light would bend, condense and reflect in ways a classically faceted stone could never achieve. The second answer to a perplexing issue was I could set the center gemstone in a bezel set tube with a hole rivet and mechanically set it in to the hole of the TorusRing.

I should add here that it's not as though from this "Eureka!" moment I just sat down and created one. I must have cut and experimented with angles and cuts in over two dozen pieces to get a really unique gemstone that was literally brilliant and beautiful to behold.

And finally, I had answered the third requirement that it could be calibrated and repeatable in the same size, shape and gemstone material. I had finally achieved what I thought was the perfect unique fantasy gemstone that would set the industry on fire. Or so I thought at his point.

So off I go to Tucson to show off my new cut – the year was 1997. To say the least, it was not a big seller. As a matter of fact the designers, the jewelry store owners and the goldsmiths all looked at it and would say, with reservation in their voice, "Interesting…"

I would get comments like, "Gee, what do you put in the hole in the center" or, "How do you set the gemstone in the center of the hole" and even, "How do you set this stone in a setting". The hardest response was, "I like the cut but my customer is so conservative". Those first couple of years the TorusRing cut was not a big seller and I experienced a lot of resistance from the jewelry industry because I believe it was so outside the box. So, person by person I would explain, "The hole in the center is to set a gemstone in, this I've left for the jeweler to create with". I would also explain how I would set a bezel set gemstone attached to a tube rivet into the TorusRing. To make it easy I would offer the service to the intrepid goldsmiths who did not trust their own skills to attempt this. Plus, I would demonstrate that setting a TorusRing cut stone is exactly the way one sets a traditional gemstone with an even girdle. No different except you can set it lower in a mounting since it is only half the depth of a conventional gemstone pavilion. Because the look and feel was so different, it was extremely hard for many jewelers to wrap their head around a cut that was completely novel and unique

So, year by year, I would win over one goldsmith/designer at a time with the concept. But this was slow going for the first four to five years. About the same time a great friend mentioned to me her brother-in-law was a patent attorney and I should show him this concept. She thought it was something I could possibly get a US utility patent for.

There are basically two types of patents someone in my industry can apply for. One is called a design patent. A design patent is based on a very definitive design and look. This would apply to maybe a certain Diamond cut such as original trillion cut. The second patent which is more difficult to get is what is defined as a utility patent. The definition of a utility patent is that the product has to be completely "Novel and Unique" in the manufacturing process as well as the end product. A completely, brand new concept in the existing field. I can tell you this really is harder than it sounds.

So, when I applied for a patent I had enough discoveries, as they are called, to give an argument that my invention of the TorusRing cut was completely novel and unique in my industry and the process of manufacturing it was unique to the current state of the art. I had two new elements, in addition to what's defined as the state of the art in gem cutting, which is the standard round brilliant . This is the gold standard that defines a brilliant cut fully reflective gemstone. The TorusRing took several new manufacturing steps, such as drilling a hole in the center and carving the inverted cone on the underside to be the internal pavilion was a step up the current technology that defines a refined brilliant cut gemstone. Thus, the end result was completely novel and unique to the field of gem cutting.

Many other gem cutters ask me all the time, "Could I, or do you think my concept is patentable?" My answer today is – it really depends. In most cases the answer is no. And in those rare discoveries of a really "novel and unique" possibly new concept then I would consider it. But then again, there is a lot to be said about "trade secrets"! We spend so many years perfecting techniques, that leaving one's cut a trade secret as to how it is produced is often the best course of action. Patents you have to expose to the light of day for others to know how you produced it. In my case applying for a patent was a smart move since it has added so much to the perceived value of the cut and brand.

The TorusRing has now found a place among the classics of gemstone cuts after a full 18 years on the market. Through the grand exposure via TV on Gemporia, it has found a huge fan base of lovers of this cut. We have sold well in excess of 60,000 over these years to the international public and trade literally in every gemstone from Amethyst and Citrine all the way to Sapphire, Ruby and Paraiba Tourmaline. It has been written and acknowledged as a new cut in the pantheon of cuts and the evolution of gem cutting.

Over the years I have had two different children from established gemstone business families come to me and ask to have a pair of TorusRing cut Sapphire earrings. These are kids that have grown up with vast exposure to the field of gems and crystals. They know a lot for their age and they could have anything because their families are in the business. My first question was to them was, "You could have anything, why a TorusRing? Is it because of the Diamond in the center?" Their answer was exactly the same, "The Diamond in the center is cool, but the real reason is I just

CARVINGS

Photo Credit:
Robert Weldon

Photo Credit:
G. Lehrer

Above An Iris Agate and Drusy Carnelian Agate carving. This Agate was found in Brazil in 2011 by Lehrer. An Iris is a certain type of Agate that when carved very thin (approx. 1.0-1.5mm) a unique phenomenon happens. With transmitted light, a rainbow diffraction of colors appear in the Agate.

Above An Iris Agate Carving, circa 1995. An Iris is a unique Agate carved very thin (approx. 1.0-1.5mm), so that when light shines through, light rainbow colors occurs. It's a phenomenal effect. **Origin:** Oregon, USA.

Photo Credit:
G. Lehrer

Photo Credit:
G. Lehrer

Above A Fantasia style carving by Lehrer, featuring Carnelian Banded Drusy Agate. Circa 1995.

Above An Oregon Rainbow Blue Clear Opal Seahorse. Weighing 64.61 cts, measuring 79x28x9mm, set with a 4mm Hot Pink Sapphire TorusRing and a vivid natural Pink Diamond eye. Set in 18k rose gold. A future Crevoshay-Lehrer Museum collection piece.

TORUSRING

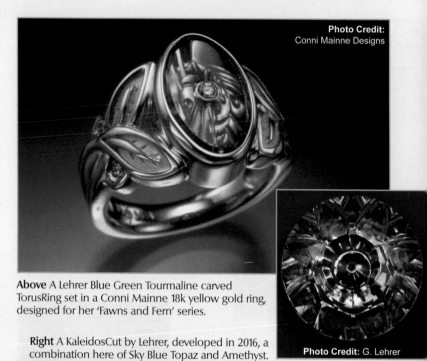

Above A Lehrer Blue Green Tourmaline carved TorusRing set in a Conni Mainne 18k yellow gold ring, designed for her 'Fawns and Fern' series.

Right A KaleidosCut by Lehrer, developed in 2016, a combination here of Sky Blue Topaz and Amethyst.

'Eye of Consciousness'
This design is composed of a concentric group of TorusRing cuts. Starting on the outside and moving in, it features a 42ct Oregon Clear Rainbow Blue Opal, with a 5.22ct Sri Lankan Fancy Hexagonal Shaped Fine Blue Sapphire TorusRing and a 0.25ct natural round Pink Sapphire TorusRing, held by a rivet of platinum and a 0.01ct Diamond.

Above A 0.84ct natura
Rainbow Tri-Color Braziliar
Paraiba Tourmaline
TorusRing, 6mm round

TORUSRING

Photo Credit:
G. Lehrer

Above A hand carved and faceted AAA Tanzanite 'Spiral Cut' oval shape TorusRing, set with a round brilliant Padparadscha Sapphire from Montana, USA, in 18k rose gold.

Photo Credit:
G. Lehrer

Above A hand carved 60ct natural Aquamarine TorusRing, set with a 3ct round brilliant cut Diamond and set in an 18k yellow gold custom pierced bezel setting necklace.

WITH STEVE

Below Glenn Lehrer and Steve Bennett appearing live on a Gemporia TV Anniversary Show, premiering one of Lehrer's Collections.

Above Steve Bennett and Glenn Lehrer at the Cruzeiro Mine, Brazil, while on a tour of 10 mines. This is when they first met and struck up their friendship, in 2011.

MAGAZINE COVERS

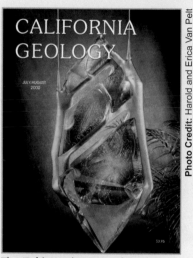

The **'Bahia'** sculpture on the cover of California Geology, July/August 2000.

The Mark Schneider **'Ballerina'** on the cover of American Jewelry magazine, January 2001.

'Dancing Angels'
This very light Pink Chalcedony and Drusy Agate carving was acquired by the Lizzadro Museum for permanent display. It was on the cover of the Lizzadro yearly publication, 2002. The Agate carving is approximately 11 inches high and is set in a sterling silver and Rainbow Obsidian base. This was their 40th anniversary cover.

A Lehrer custom carved and designed Drusy Carnelian Agate and Lehrer 18k yellow gold and Pearl necklace, on the cover of Basel Magazine, May 2000.

MAGAZINE COVERS

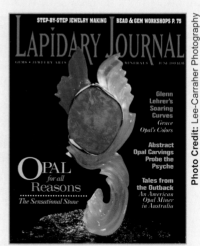

On the cover of the GIA periodical, Gems and Gemology, along with three other pieces of jewelry designed by Paula Crevoshay. On the right side is a 37.04ct Brazilian Orange Fire Opal TorusRing, 30.6mm, carved by Lehrer.

'Opal Dragon'
An interwoven three-piece carving, two pieces of Chrysoprase and one Silicated Azurite piece surround a Lightning Ridge Black Opal, all assembled by tap and die screws in 18k yellow gold. This was custom designed and fabricated for a private collection. It made its way on to the cover of Lapidary Journal, June 1995.

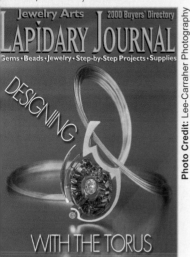

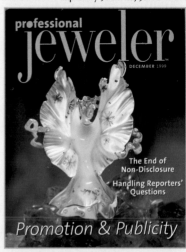

A Gordon Aatlo 18k yellow gold design using Lehrer's TorusRing Eclipse cut in Ametrine, on the cover of Lapidary Journal's Tucson Buyers Guide, February 2000.

Mark Schneider's **'Angel'** with a Lehrer carved Dendritic Agate, shown here on Professional Jeweler, December 1999.

AWARD WINNERS

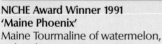

NICHE Award Winner 1991
'Maine Phoenix'
Maine Tourmaline of watermelon, red and green, 179cts, a 0.52ct trillion Diamond and 18k yellow gold. On permanent exhibition at the Maine Mineral and Gem Museum.
www.mainemineralmuseum.org
This piece was also featured on the cover of America Jewelry Magazine, October 1990.

AGTA 1998
Cutting Edge Award Winner
A 4.02ct Montana Golden Sapphire TorusRing, with an 82.16ct African Blue Chalcedony carving, and a 124.49ct Black Drusy Agate carving. First place in carving category.
See Page 2 for More
Information on This Carving

2005 AGTA Cutting Edge Winner

Glenn Lehrer
Lehrer Designs

1st Place
Carving Category

Photo Credit: American Gem Traders Association

AGTA 2005
Cutting Edge Winner
Carving of a 194ct Aquamarine, carved and faceted. First place.

AWARD WINNERS

AGTA 2016 Cutting Edge Award Winner
A 48.46ct Lightning Ridge Black Opal, carved cameo style to expose the various different color layers of fire in the stone. Second place in carving category.

AGTA 1991 Spectrum Award Winner
A 42ct shield shape Opal, with Chrysoprase bullet cabs, Black Jade, Rainbow Labradorite, Diamonds and 18k yellow gold. Set in a hand woven 18k yellow gold chain. Third place winner, Spectrum.

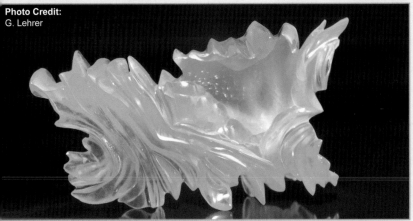

AGTA 1995 Cutting Edge Award Winner
Arizona Botryoidal Silicated Chrysocolla and Malachite carving, 75.09cts. Second place.

TRAVEL AND FAMILY

Above Glenn with his new found friend, Mohamed, a Berber Merchant, hunting for gem rough in the back country of Morocco, 2016.

Above Glenn with the head Berber Tribal Leader of the Moroccan Amethyst Mine

Above Ruth Lehrer, Glenn's mother at her 100th birthday party in 2015

Below Glenn with his wife Sharon in 2016, living in Marin County, California, USA. Happily married for 35 years

Above 'The Boys' circa 1960. From front to back, youngest brother Harvey, the middle is Glenn, then older brother Wayne and their father Bill at the back.

love how the light plays in the TorusRing cut. I've never seen this before." The TorusRing is known for bending light in such unique and novel ways. Something a round brilliant cut just can't reproduce. It's the cone in the center which is curved to condense light into a thin beam of light reflecting back to the outside pavilion creating an almost Iris of the Eye effect. It is like it's primordial and archetypal in the brilliance of the light.

It is a never-ending evolution in the art. Just recently I've come up with the QuasarCut in its diversity of shapes and then the KaleidosCut series furthering the evolution of the cut.

The future is ripe with new beginnings, ideas and manifestations of beauty. After 40 years, I feel I'm just warming up, not slowing down. I literally can't wait to see what lies around the next corner of my creative process.

12

CO-BRAND

· Co-Creating with Some of the Most Talented Jewelry Designers in Modern History

"Compensatory genius is when one brilliant mind makes up the shortcomings of another brilliant one".
Eric Weiner, Geography of Genius

Co-creativity is a unique dance of complex elements coming together, fitting with one another like a jigsaw puzzle and succeeding as a team to create something far greater than an individual could do on one's own. Buckminster Fuller defines synergy thus: "Synergetics is the empirical study of systems in transformation, with an emphasis on total system behavior unpredicted by the behavior of any isolated components, including humanity's role as both participant and observer."

Minerals could not be more definitive to demonstrate the Principles of Synergistics. Minerals, or more specifically gem quality minerals, are the very expression and finalized state of being that have gone through tremendous transformational change. Minerals come into being, born from diverse elements and extreme conditions that create something greater than a single element can be on its own in most cases. There are those rare Native elements that can form into a mineral by itself, i.e. gold and Diamond. But in nearly all cases minerals - and more specifically gemstones – are a complex relationship of more than two elements that come together in a geometrically repeating symmetrical pattern that creates something far more than any of the elements could form on their own. Sounds metaphorically not unlike relationships between us as humans, seeking and being in relationships to one another as couples, groups and nations of humanity. I believe they are not as far apart as they appear just on the surface of its physicality. Nature and the universe is the master in this art of co-creativity.

For individuals, to co-create with Nature is one outpouring of this drive. It appears to magically arise from inside our soul and yearn to be expressed. Then to co-create with another, as an individual or team of individuals, seems to be the very destiny and drive in many of us. From a husband and wife partnership, to complex corporate teams and cultures of people and governments, co-creativity is the fuel that drives success around a project or a greater long term accomplishment. It is where one can look back on history and see a renaissance of a certain culture and period of time in history rise up and shine as a beacon of humanity's ingenuity and never-ending quest for beauty in our lives. A major outpouring and flourishing of the arts, literature and sciences within that culture and historical time. This is how we as a planetary race have evolved over the last 200,000 years on earth. Constantly building upon previous inventions and ingenuity. Crystals and minerals could be metaphorically held as archetypes to this very pattern in our drive to achieve, accomplish and evolve as the human race on this planet. Something for us all to contemplate and use to ignite our imaginations.

My most co-creative relationship that has been a big part of my living life is my marriage to my wife, Sharon. We started out as a couple, went through years of learning to communicate, to trust and constantly expand our beliefs and attitude to what love is and means in partnership. Becoming the very best of friends to one another, to then further the evolution and definition of our relationship by becoming business partners. We've done it all except have kids. It was a life choice we both made early on. So, in a small way the world became our surrogate child. The nephews, nieces, close friends' kids and the world beyond our culture, I feel we have jumped in to learn and hopefully be part of a better world by contributing in our own unique small way by bringing more beauty and meaning to our world. That old saying that a marriage gets better like a fine wine can be so true. Over these 35 years of our marriage, our bond is greater today than it has even been. Don't get me wrong, we had our moments of pain, struggle, fear and failures together in the normal cause of any loving relationship. From these triumphs, our bond has only strengthened and our love has ever expanded and deepened in ways we only glimpsed when we first fell in love.

One would believe I live for my art. This is only the half of the truth. Just as important as my art, if not even more so, is my personal and professional relationships. I've come to realize that a relationship with others who are creative and ingenious is often more important to me than the actual finished piece of art work. From my marriage to creating a piece of art with another, to my professional business partnerships, to serving a greater cause as a board member or trustee of non-profit organizations are also extremely ripe areas in my life to be creative and look for solutions. I love to be in relationships with others and co-create in all its various dimensions from the art to the ideals put to action.

In many ways, I actually feel my art is my vehicle, the form, and all my relationships are the function to my life. I feel I derive more from living a fun creative life with art then just doing the solo artist model. Starting with my family, my wife and I have been driven to have co-creative relationships in the creation of art and related business partnerships in the Gem and Jewelry Industry. Every one of these relationships feeds me as much, if not more, than just creating another beautiful object. This chapter is about co-creativity in the creation of gemstone and jewelry with another. A tandem or team effort where the outcome is far greater then I could imagine or create on my own.

Lawrence Stoller was my first real partner on this level of working and succeeding together as two artists coming together and creating something far greater than either of us could have done alone. We taught each other so much on the art of co-creativity. Together we learned the dos and don'ts to succeeding. Not only were we creating something that had never existed before in Gem Art (see the chapter on Bahia) but simultaneously we struggled in partnership, faced each other down in loud, strong conversations and both grew as individuals because of our partnership. We often joked with one another that as we chiseled away at the crystal, we were chiseling and polishing each other to become better more balanced individuals. I know I am a better person and more evolved as a soul because of our joint partnership as co-artists over 11 years working together. Lawrence: you were my first Guru to the Art and Principle of Co-creating with another around art projects. But it was also more than just Lawrence and I together. Sunni, Lawrence's wife and Sharon, my wife, were just as involved in this co-creative process. Though they did not do any of the actual work, they were constantly there in the process keeping Lawrence's and my egos in check. Plus, they were definitely involved in many of the creative decisions that needed to be made during the process of cutting and the promotion after the completion of the particular pieces.

Then along comes Uli Pauly from Idar-Oberstein, Germany and our co-creation of the Visionary Artist. Here, for the first time I've been told, a second-generation Master Cameo Carver is co-creating with an American with no tradition. We made a map where the unknown self-taught Gem Artist cross fertilized with a trained Master who had 500 years of tradition behind his upbringing. It was exciting and exhilarating and we both share our deep gratitude and appreciation for what each of us brought to the table when it came to creating an art piece as well as managing the business side of it in partnership. Uli: your grace and integrity as a person and an artist further honed my co-creativity skills and instilled a trust that success can come elegantly and graciously. As like the relationship with Lawrence and Sunni, both my wife, Sharon and Uli's wife, Gaby, were there in full attendance to help guide and engage in the business decisions and give wisdom along the way. Again, another pair of couples co-creating around the art.

One of the true facts is that the colored gemstone and jewelry business is full of Mom and Pop companies that thrive and in many ways, drive our industry. And in both of my cases it was not just about creating an art piece, but the process as a group and the spiritual base in which we all held as one, was a powerful glue and catalyst for some amazing arts work. A depth of relationship one seeks often for fulfillment, we have managed to create and thrive on. Both with Uli and Lawrence, I know I've grown and matured in ways I know I could never achieve as an individual artist working in solitude. Plus, it's just too darn fun doing it with another.

The general theme over the centuries is that a jewelry designer will purchase a gemstone from a dealer, never really knowing the creator of the stone. They buy it because they are inspired by what they see in that dealer's inventory, never knowing or being able to discuss the piece with the creator of that gemstone. What is different here is I have a direct and very personal relationship with the designer often before, during and after they have completed their work. I have stated previously that in most cases my artwork is half completed. In this I mean: I do a Gem Art piece keeping in mind a designer needs to come by and be inspired to co-create with my work. I have to leave room for another to see something more and not just a stand-alone art piece to be place on some mantle or framed. For me, this is exciting in that I get to leave a bit of magic and mystery with so many of my gemstone carvings to inspire to see more than what's there before their eyes.

I am so deeply grateful to the many co-creative Jewelry Designers I worked with over these many decades. In this chapter I will focus on seven jewelry designers I have co-created with and feel best express this sense of something more because of our joint co-creation. With each individual, the process is unique and different in that we are all very different people, with unique styles and processes in which we create. Our co-creative process is unique to each of our relationships with each other. The end results will reflect how the same gemstone carving can be seen uniquely with each of these artists and the outcome original to each of theirs and my styles in combination with one another.

In this chapter I share with you my insights of working individually with each of them. I have also asked each of the seven to write something from their vantage point what it is like to co-create with my carvings and gemstones and to work in tandem as a co-creative team.

The seven I have invited are: Paula Crevoshay, Mark Schneider, Kent Raible, Yehouda Sakethou, Manuj Goyal, Stephan Gunning and the late Gordon Aatlo (his daughter Christine will contribute) to share their experiences, insights and feeling of what it is like to work with my carvings and co-create with a Gem Artist. This will be a sharing of co-creativity and you can see in the photos section the diversity of designs and styles that have been created by the interactive collaboration of Designer Jeweler and Gem Artist.

But before we jump into the personal individual reflections from each of the seven artists, there are several elements and principles that I have learned that are essential for a successful relationship in co-creativity around our art form.

Below are the seven principles, but not necessarily in any order, and by no means every principle is called upon here, that is required for a successful co-creative process and project. But I feel the seven below all have to be present for the co-creativity to give birth to exceptional gem art pieces and for the relationship to become more.

Principle #1

Respect and Honor. You must absolutely respect others for the unique skills and knowledge they bring to the table. See all as equal and recognize the gifts and talents they bring to the project. Each individual has something unique to bring to the creation.

Principle #2

Humility. Each individual must have a degree of humility. Meaning you must remain open to ideas that are either outside what you're thinking or you may differ with. Put your ego to the side and listen and respect the other's opinions, whether you agree or not. Stay open to something new and be willing to change your belief system mid-course because of the dialogue that arises during the process.

Principle #3

Be Yourself 100%. Be 100% authentic. Show up and be yourself and allow your personal genius to shine and contribute to the process. Not to have one dominate over the other, but for there to exist a real sense of dominion in partnership. Be honest about what you can do and what you can't. Your thoughts and opinions matter. Don't lie to yourself or others. This is being authentic with a personal sense of authority knowing your thoughts and feelings matter. This is real co-creativity, when each one comes from this place of personal dominion.

Principle #4

Courage. Have the courage to stand up and speak your truth in light of the direction you see the group or team are moving towards. Tell the truth.

Principle #5

Agreement. The project does not proceed until all involved in the decision-making agree 100% as to the next step moving forward. This to me is one of the most important principles that create a successful creation in a co-creative process with another. This one principle, Lawrence and I established early on in our relationship, long before we ever started Bahia. We called upon this principle over and over again when it came time to navigate the many ups and downs in the creation of Bahia. This one principle I would say kept us on track and focused from the beginning to the completion of stone, as well moving forward until the final sale of Bahia to GIA happened.

Principle #6

Have Trust. Trust in self, others and the dream, even when there does not seem to be a light at the end of a tunnel. This is a hard one for a group or couple to hang in there when it appears in complete chaos or lost as to the viability of the ultimate goal or dream. It's easy to hang in there when everything is going great. It's a real challenge and testimony to a powerful co-creative team to hang in there when the going gets rough. During times where the team can't see the light at the end of the tunnel or major adversity is staring you down the barrel of a gun, being able to hang in this liminal space as a group calls for real strength that will often test the bond of the relationship to its power to hold together and move forward.

Principle #7
Celebrate All Along the Way. When one starts out, during certain bench marks in the unfolding of the project and of course upon completion or financial success of the project. Reward each other in the successes, in the embarking, along the way and upon completion. This builds unity and team focus.

The Art of Paula Crevoshay

My personal insight into working with Paula Crevoshay over 20 plus years:

When art historians look back at the late 20th and early 21st century they will see the Renaissance of beauty in carved gemstones and jewelry designs; an expression of a new level of synergy between human creativity and the mineral kingdom. Between Gem Carver and Jewelry Designer, something brand new, never seen or imagined before.

Paula Crevoshay is one of those rare designers I believe that has captured this period with her extraordinary use of colored gemstones and a global fusion of styles.

Paula's palette of colored gemstones is vibrant and radiates the very passion and excitement for life that her spirit and soul give out into the world. Her designs in jewelry reflect many cultures that speak of her own life's journey. When one beholds her jewelry collection one can't help but feel a deeper sense of beauty and love that lies within the core of Nature's wonder. She captures this beauty in her work, frozen in time for generations to be inspired by.

Paula has been working with my gemstone carvings for several decades. When she approached me with the concept of doing a rare museum collection using my gemstone carvings with her jewelry designs, I knew together as co-artists the final outcome would be a new transcendent expression of the synergy between gemstone and jewelry art.

I have always loved how she interprets my style of impressionism in gemstone art. Paula elevates my carvings to levels that inspire me to stretch my creativity to new heights.

As a co-creative team, Paula and I have taken synergy to new heights of innovation in a single artist expression of beauty.

Paula Crevoshay's Personal Insight Working With Lehrer

The day I first saw Glenn Lehrer and his carvings I was totally amazed at the way he bends the light. I immediately had to have some to work with.

What his work does to me is like yoga. I literally have to stretch into myself in my art brain. We have collaborated on many projects over three decades now. His extraordinary works continue to morph into new untraveled horizons. It's like he time travels into the light and returns with his treasures to bare. My collaborations have always been uplifting and mind expanding. Sometimes I give him some of my sketches to design and he still blows me away with how he translates the light into wearable art! We are working on a special project together that we both feel will be a pinnacle in our synergies over these decades. Asking me to describe my favorites is like asking a mother to pick her favorite child. I love them all!

Glenn appeals to my female sensibilities and aesthetics that blend so beautifully with my style as a fine jewelry artist. His works synthesize through my heart chakra and creative juices blend his light with mine. His pieces become goddesses, sea creatures, empresses, flying fish, imps and fairies to suns of other universes in our combined works. He taps the same archetypes that inspire me and my vision into other worlds.

I am so blessed to know him and have such intimate access and trust to his vivid and brilliant inspirations. We are spiritual art siblings. I hope to be working for several more decades with this wizard of the light.

The Mastery of Stephan Gunning, Goldsmith

My personal insight into working with Stephan Gunning:

Stephan Gunning is one of the most talented master goldsmiths I've ever worked side by side with. In this day and age where almost everything in jewelry manufacturing has gone digital, old school goldsmiths like Stephan are a rare find. His mastery in almost every aspect of traditional goldsmithing, from hand fabrication of gold, stone setting and wax work is par-excellence. Though I have a basic background in precious metal fabrication and wax work I've come to count on Stephan to be the consummate master when it comes to creating one of a kind pieces in our studio at Lehrer Designs, Inc.

Working almost daily alongside Stephan at the bench has been a real gift for me. I've come to lean on his knowledge and experience when we create unique designs in precious metal with my gem cuts. We have this most fluid ability to bounce ideas off one another, discuss the best way to execute some of the most difficult techniques of setting my stones in the jewelry pieces, to create very unique one-off pieces for Lehrer Designs customers.

At Lehrer Designs we've been known to be the last resort when no one else in the industry can do it. Companies and individuals turn to us to be the ones to pull it off when no one else is willing or able. Those hard to execute designs between Stephan's and my combined 80 years of experience, we're able to pull it off with elegance and excellence. It is rare to be able to work alongside such a talented goldsmith like Stephan where he is open to suggestion and is able to brainstorm how we are going to pull it off or do it differently than tradition. In other words, so many experienced craftspeople are fixed on how to do a certain skill.

With Stephan we flow so well together and are constantly relying on one another's abilities to create unique one-of-a -kind jewelry pieces. With Stephan, I can make suggestions on various ways to achieve the same end and he is completely humble and of an open mind within his knowledge and skill. We seem to blend so perfectly and fulfill each other's abilities and skills. Together there has not been a piece we have not been able to do or create with our combined artistry and mastery of goldsmithing. When it comes to jewelry designs and my gem cuts we make the perfect team at Lehrer Designs studios.

Stephan Gunning's Personal Insight Working With Lehrer

I was aware of the beauty of Glenn Lehrer's gem carvings before I had ever started working with him, by seeing his craftsman at trade shows and through Susan Bickford, an Independent Jewelry Appraiser.

In 1998, I had just come back from Guatemala with some of the most stunning and rare Jadeite Jade that Ventana Mining had ever discovered: The Lost Jade of the Olmec Culture. We needed the material to be worked by the best Gem Carver and Designer, and everyone within Ventana Mining agreed that Glenn was a perfect choice.

It was then we had our first collaboration; we discussed the best ways to bring the vibrant colors out of the Jadeite. His work on our material without a doubt showcased the quality which elevated the status of Guatemala Jadeite to a world-class gem.

A couple of years after Ventana Mining started working with Glenn, my fiancé, Susan Bickford, became terminally ill with cancer. I stopped working in the Palo Alto area and relocated to Marin County to take care of her for the last year of her life. During that time of hardship and loss, my relationship with Glenn changed.

Our collaboration now was incorporating all gems in creating jewelry.

The cathartic nature working with Glenn on dynamic new jewelry pieces is truly a healing process that opened up many avenues of growth in designs. It begins in many ways; often it is started with someone's request for a distinctive new piece and is where we get to tap into the emotions of jewelry and discover areas that excite and stimulate the senses. Blending the different techniques of fabrication and casting, and the incorporation of stone settings and beautifully carved gemstones.

There will be sketches drawn, and the ideas get bounced around on how best to achieve the concepts. It is in this back and forth of ideas and approaches that one finds healing and the designs coming into formation. We can then move to carving a wax to see how it looks in three dimensions or work up the prototype to see how the lines flow and fit together. Again, we revisit the design and discuss how it makes Glenn and I feel, and what we still need to do to produce it, so it captures the emotions that we felt at the beginning. This is my favorite part: unraveling the unknown and watching it unfold into the masterpiece that leads Glenn and I into an epiphany in the design.

Collaboration is the center stone of solving problems and the basis of our relationship.

We continue to move forward in this creative business producing spectacular jewelry and open to the next challenge.

The Art of Mark Schneider

My personal insight into working with Mark Schneider:

Mark Schneider is one of the most recognized jewelry designers alive today. He has won numerous Spectrum awards for his designs and his work is on display is some of America's finest museums including the Smithsonian Museum in Washington, DC.

Mark was one of the very first designers that was willing to work with my Fantasia carvings back in the late 80s. I can still see him walking into my showroom in Tucson and very closely studying my work. He was exactly the perfect artist I had dreamt of that would be willing to create unique one-off jewelry pieces with my Fantasia carvings. He would seize the challenge and get really excited about working with my carvings.

So many jewelry designers at the time kept telling me that my carvings were too complicated, too much of a completed design that they felt that there was very little they could do with my carvings in their jewelry designs. Not so with Mark. Mark Schneider was one of the first to see exactly what I intended with my Fantasia carvings, in that they were half done pieces of art waiting for a designer like him to come along and lift it up into unique, one-off designs the industry had not seen before. Mark was very different in that he allowed me to create what I wanted in stone and then he would come along and be inspired and create outside the traditional box of jewelry designs. Other designers like to get very much involved in the gem design. But Mark always allowed me to create what

I dreamt, then he would come along and envision something so original and unique.

With my carvings, he is able to dream up that impressionistic style of a bird, a butterfly and even a ballerina: exactly what I always dreamt could be done with my Fantasia series. Mark was the perfect designer I intended for my work. As I have mentioned before I always feel my carvings are only half done, purposely waiting for someone like Mark to come along and dream up ideas that are completely novel and unique. Our combined work together received so much acclaim we have appeared on four major jewelry magazine covers with our combined work; won awards; and have exhibited at museums. We continue to create those unique dancing ballerinas and angels that have graced these magazine covers. Each one unique and one of a kind in the completed form.

Mark Schneider's Personal Insight Working With Lehrer

I have had many of Glenn's stones in my personal collection for over 15 years and each time I look at them, I see something new to create – something that I haven't seen before. I see a stone that I have looked at dozens of times, and where I didn't see it before, this time I see a ballerina, a bird, or the rising of the phoenix. I love Glenn's work because it is very organic, which really follows my typical design style. He has this rare talent of bringing out the most beautiful and unique characteristics of each gemstone.

I love using Glenn's stones for competition pieces because when I design a competition or project piece, not only is the design judged, but the stone is also judged within the piece. In these cases, I always start with the gemstone first. Whether out of my own collection, or working with a particular cutter, I find the most successful pieces begin by letting the stone talk to me and lead me in the direction of the design. My mind is inspired by gemstone cutters like Glenn, who take a more personal interest in the stones they sell. Their work is much more than just getting return on the investment from a piece of rough. It is putting their personal imprint on the gemstone and signing it.

When I allow the gemstone cutter to cut the stone his own way, I am giving him the freedom to create the gemstone in the image that he feels best represents the stone. Just like I allow the gemstone to talk to me when I am creating my designs, the cutter must let the gemstone talk to him so he knows what shape it should take. I like the gemstone cutter to be as creative as he can without any influence from me, and then it's my job to take his stone and create a design that showcases his art, as well as my design.

It takes 3 elements to make a winning design – what nature creates (the rough), what the gemstone cutter can add to the stone, and the design, which is what I feel is the best presentation of the stone. Working with an artist like Glenn adds a unique quality to the final piece of jewelry. It's my job to bring out the qualities of Glenn's work as well as the natural beauty of the stone.

The Art and Mastery of Kent Raible

My personal insight into working with Kent Raible:

Kent Raible is one of the most amazing goldsmiths and granulation artists living today. Kent is an American who received his training in goldsmithing in Germany. Germany is known for their excellent training in the age-old craft of fine metalsmithing in a town in the Black Forest of Germany called Pforzheim. Similar to the schools in Idar-Oberstein where one goes to gain their master degree in the craft. In this day and age of computers, his work is done the age-old way by hand forging and forming.

Granulation is where you place tiny multiple small fine gold or silver beads to the surface of the metal to create various patterns of design on the surface of the metal. Kent even using the age-old technique of a blow torch to attach the tiny spheres of gold to the surface of the work. Similar to playing a wind instrument where one learns to breathe, in a circular motion the correct oxygen is added to the fuel to create the correct heat that melts the solder and attaches the metal spheres to the surface of the work. It is an ancient Etruscan (700 to 500 BC) art form in very fine gold or silver that was rediscovered and developed by masters like Kent. Aside from his gold work, he continues to teach and train new goldsmiths in this ancient art form in metal.

I love working with Kent. He has been working with my gemstone carvings and TorusRing designs for over 20 years. His antique design style in high gold purity granulation and my carvings just blend seamlessly with one another.

The TorusRing cut is one of those gem cut styles that just blends with motifs of antiquity as well as very modern styles of today. Aside from the many one-of-a-kind pieces he has done with my TorusRing, we have also created a few one off unique carvings for some of his best customers. The most recent was an Aquamarine where I carved a waterfall motif with hollow concave chambers into which he then inserted another colored gemstone and a prayer wheel design that turns with movement.

I love working side by side with Kent in that he gives me a basic concept and then lets me interrupt it as I see fit or the gem material dictates. His work is what we in the industry call "top drawer". I am truly honored to be part of his work that I know collectors far and wide seek out his work. A modern-day master still practicing old world techniques. A rarity in this day and age.

Kent Raible's Personal Insight Working With Lehrer

Glenn and I go way back, as we both lived in Marin County, California when we were just starting out in the 70s. We were very aware of each other as we developed our skills and started winning awards; I would say there has always been a mutual admiration of each other's skill and artistry.

When Glenn came out with the TorusRing, I was immediately hooked – the symmetry of the cut works well with my designs, and I love the softness of the brilliance he achieves with the cuts on the concave facet underneath, a sort of half cabochon, half faceted look. And then there is that wonderful hole in the middle, perfect for that brilliant center focal point! The TorusRing was perfect for my ring designs, as the overall depth for a large stone was so much less than a conventional faceted stone, so I could get a lot more of a statement with a lot less height. These unique gems are the perfect match for my unique gold techniques, and I have been using them for decades.

Glenn is also great at fulfilling custom requests, and over the years I have called him to help me with some really unusual jobs. Most recently, a client's request led to a major pendant/ necklace commission in which I had Glenn use an Aqua crystal with a natural prismatic crystalline surface (from his private stash). He carved a waterfall on one side and also made a large cylindrical cut in the back to my specifications. I inserted a large, rotating gold and gem encrusted (and also removable to be worn separately) Prayer Wheel into that cylindrical cut in the back of the crystal, and held it in position top and bottom with two cityscape caps of platinum, gold and various gems, many of which Glenn also cut to my specs. As the piece is worn, the Prayer Wheel in the back rolls back and forth with the movement of the wearer, causing an ever-changing distorted reflection through the natural facets of the Aqua crystal. I entitled the piece World of Vanishing Illusions.

It's been a great pleasure and honor to work with Glenn all these years, and I look forward to the next project!

The Art of Yehouda Sakethou

My personal insight into working with Yehouda Sakethou, Yael Designs:

Though Yehouda and I have just started to create works together over the last couple of years, it is already not without major benchmark achievement. I am thrilled to be working with him. His work has received numerous awards and honors. He is an amazing designer and he is constantly pushing me to stretch what I thought was possible in stone when the two of us get together. We are flying outside the box.

Sometimes it takes someone from outside my box to stretch and get me to interrupt my Gem Art in new and refreshing ways. To push my own belief systems beyond the boundaries of what I've done in the past. I feel we both admire one another in this way. Yehouda has a way of dreaming outside the box and come to me with his wild and crazy ideas. Instead of saying it's not possible, I take the challenge and give it my all to try and achieve his vision of the stone. I love him for this. After 40 years in my craft, it's designers like Yehouda who come along and force me to come up with new and refreshing approaches to stone. One often needs ideas from outside one's world to go and create in exciting new ways. Yehouda is this kind of guy. I just love co-creating with him because of this. Together we achieve something neither of us could do it alone. My working relationship with him is always fun and exhilarating, plus we have become good friends on top of our working partnership. Best of both worlds.

Yehouda Sakethou's Personal Insight Working With Lehrer

Working with Glenn Lehrer has been a tremendous experience. As the CEO of Yael Designs, I've collaborated with other prominent jewelers over the years, but knew Glenn only from his wide reputation as a legendary gem cutter.

For two years, I've dreamt about creating a piece where one gemstone would be set inside another, but when I approached other people with the idea, they laughed in my face. Then, I finally reached out to Glenn. I knew that if he couldn't do it, no one could. To my surprise and relief, instead of saying my dream was impossible, he got excited about my idea and said that it would be a challenge that he wanted to take on.

In the jewelry industry, there are a lot people who do the talk, so I tend to be skeptical when working with new people. But when we set out to work together, Glenn turned out to be both extremely knowledgeable and modest. He patiently taught me things I didn't know about gems and walked me through every step of developing our vision. There was a lot of synergy and back and forth between us as we made the piece. In fact, in the process of working together, we came up with a new idea that took the stone-in-stone idea even further into a totally new experiment with color reflection. I think the best outcome of any collaboration is when a new idea is borne because of it.

It is rare that you can combine a grand vision with an equally grand skill set, but that's exactly what we found in our partnership. Together, Glenn and I created the first ever piece of jewelry where one stone is set inside another. We called it Sentience and it received a lot of attention in the jewelry industry. It also turned out to be the beginning of a longer partnership. After working so well on the first piece, we decided to turn this new jewelry-making technology into a whole patented collection.

I know that without Glenn, my dream would have stayed just that – a dream. Instead, it went from a dream to a challenge to reality and now to a business, all thanks to a man who was willing to believe.

The Art of the Late Gordon Aatlo

My personal insight into working with the late Gordon Aatlo:

The late Gordon Aatlo was one of those designers who came to me early in my career. He immediately showed appreciation for my work when many other designers would admire it, but not commit to working with my stones. This was not so with Gordon. He is another one of those old-world craftsmen who had a tremendous command of the skills that is required from a classically trained goldsmith. Though Gordon was trained in old world skills, his designs are far from vintage in look. He was a very versed designer, aside from his skills as a metalsmith. His work is very modern and elegantly original in concept. There are great designers who have others execute the actual work and there are great goldsmiths who are not that talented in designing. Gordon not only could design artistically but create the work par excellence all on his own. It's unique to see both skills in one person.

From the get go, we hit the ground running together back in the early 90s. His designs with my TorusRing cut was immediately a marriage made in heaven. He was one of those designers who immediately fell in love with the TorusRing cut when others were still standing on the sidelines. I can emphatically state that designers like Gordon put the TorusRing cut on the radar of the jewelry industry and the public at large. His clients just went crazy for our joint work. Together our collaborative work has been shown on the cover of national trade magazines and major museum exhibitions. His eye for detail was amazing. Sometimes the simplest looking designs are actually the most complicated to pull off. His designs were minimal in appearance but complicated in concept. His work had a refined architectural appearance and beauty to it. Simple but complicated. A really hard ability to pull off. This was Gordon. My stones and his designs just melded perfectly together. When Steve Bennett of Gemporia first ask me to appear on his TV channels back in 2011 with my one-off top drawer pieces, I immediately turned to Gordon to contribute his finished pieces with my carvings to my first debut show on Gemporia. They are what helped launch my long-standing relationship with Gemporia.

Though he has passed on, his family continues to work with my stones in the many of the designs Gordon molded for production. We would sit together and co-create in so many creative ways for hours on end. It was Gordon who first inspired me to create the Eclipse cut TorusRing design that made it on the cover of Lapidary Journal. I miss working with him along with his gentle nature.

Christine Aatlo Recalls Gordon Aatlo's Personal Insight Working With Lehrer

In the 1950s, at the beginning of Gordon Aatlo's jewelry career, the fascination with designer gemstone began. At that time, not many gemstones were being produced with unusual, one of a kind shapes. Seeking to create something different, and at the same time, challenging his skills, Gordon began using Rococo cuts from Brazil, which peaked the interest of jewelry lovers.

There was a small, select audience for work in Gem Art in the 1980s and 1990s, but because of his influences, a new generation of distinctive gem carvers was born, including Glenn Lehrer who presented an innovative point of view in gem designs. In the late winter of February 1998, at the Tucson gem shows, Gordon Aatlo introduced his designs to the worldwide gemstone community. Showing his pieces that blurred tradition boundaries, he offered something different, which to his point of view, you either liked it or you didn't. That difference is what attracted Glenn and Gordon to each other's work and started the exploration of collaboration with one another.

The challenge initially for Gordon with Glenn's famous TorusRing was the signature hole in the center of the gem. Working in small series, Gordon began creating a new form of design, one to complement the beauty of Glenn's intricate and detailed gemstones.

Many hours of sketching and experimentation began, while Glenn and Gordon brainstormed, each giving the other their own perspective of not only design, but also material selections. The first set of designs were rings using round TorusRing cuts, with very clean lines and minimal diamond accents.

Glenn expanded his designs in the TorusRing series to include pear shapes, trilliants and oblong Elliptical cuts. As was Gordon's custom, he always waited for the gem to speak to him and the design would involve, making Glenn's work the focal point of the piece of jewelry. Through the years, Gordon would commission Glenn to cut smaller TorusRings to fit into larger TorusRings, and another successful series was created.

The appeal of the talents of these two became well known, with their work together highly anticipated, forming the beginning of a renaissance of gem and jewelry art. No two gems by Glenn or jewelry design by Gordon with Glenn's masterpieces were ever identical.

It is said that lightning strikes only once, but in the case of these artists, the lightning continued in many forms for more than 15 years in different forms of design and artistry and a true meeting of the minds of the concept of beauty, talent and courage to introduce to the world, another art form. Today, an original Lehrer/Aatlo collaborative piece is highly collectable and a highly sought treasure. Gordon's designs with Glenn's art are preserved by his family and continues to be an extremely popular combination of two extraordinary visionaries.

The Master of Manufacturing, Manuj Goyal, Jewelry Manufacturer of Pink City, India

My personal insight into working with Manuj Goyal:

Long before I knew who Manuj Goyal was, apparently he knew who I was. For years, I would go to the GIA campus and give a general talk about gem carving and show the gemology students my work. I found out much later, Manuj was one of those in the sea of eyes looking at me from the audience. He later told me once we started to work together, that he dreamt someday he would work with me when he heard me speak at GIA. It's always amazing how one's intention can create one's reality. He got what he wished for.

It was not until around 2008, when my business was falling apart during the Great Recession, that I turned to my good friend Yianni Melas and asked him if he knew of anyone who would be willing to hire me for my gem cutting expertise. I was looking to stay afloat during difficult times and knew my skill sets would be a real bonus for a company somewhere in the world. Yianni immediately set up a call between Manuj and I to connect and possibly work together. However, the timing was not right at the time so nothing came of it then.

It was not until Steve Bennett and I connected in Brazil in 2010, when we were trying to decide how to create my special gem cuts that Manuj's name came again to light. Steve said at the time, "I know of only one person in Jaipur who could possibly do your cut. His name is Manuj Goyal." To Steve's surprise I said I knew who he was because I'd had a talk with him a few years earlier via our mutual friend, Yianni.

One of the critical issues of taking my work overseas and training cutters how to do very difficult techniques, is that now I'm exposing them to new skills that could easily be taken and used for their own purpose. We have a term in the industry call, "Bleed Out." Years earlier I had attempted to produce my work in a factory in China. I experienced a loss in that many of my stones were returned broken and their manager left the factory and attempted to take my cut with him. One of the cores of why my relationship in Jaipur with Manuj has been such a huge success is that he fiercely guards my work and we only have a very small, select handful of trained cutters knowing the complete process. I love working with Manuj because his factory is state of the art in gem cutting and jewelry manufacturing. Though Manuj does not produce his own designs, his core is being a top notch subcontractor for large manufacturers worldwide. He knows that if there is bleed out it hurts his core business as much as it hurts the designer he's working with.

Though I'm good at creating unique one-of-a-kind cuts, Manuj's expertise is being able to take these unique cuts and reproduce them in quantity. This is no small feat. It's easy to produce one by hand but to then turn around and cut hundreds, one needs to reverse engineer the process so each pieces is calibrated and uniform in size and quality. Manuj is a master at this. I just love working with him and his factory. We have produced thousands now in the 5 years we have been working together. I go to Jaipur 3-4 times a year to work with him and develop my cuts and jewelry for manufacturing purposes. I stay with him in his home and have been adopted as a family member as an "Uncle". This is the Indian way.

I can look back to when I was in India 40 years earlier on my spiritual quest to now, knowing my time in India was the primer to my time now working in India alongside him and his staff. I know the culture well and am very comfortable being there and working in his factory.

Another reason why I love working with his factory is that it is completely compliant in labor laws and environmental impact. I feel that my product is trade free and those producing them are making a fair and good wage. This has become extremely important in today's market place that one's brand and products are completely compliant because here in the West consumers demand this more and more.

Manuj Goyal's Personal Insight Working With Lehrer

As a student at GIA, I had a keen desire to focus my life in the world of gemstones. It's also where I first heard about Glenn when he came for a mentoring session, lighting up our minds with his immense knowledge, creativity and vision. His masterpiece, Bahia (living at the GIA), was a constant physical reminder of the genius Glenn is. To be able to speak to someone as accomplished, was a dream. Our collaboration can be chronicled by Neil Gaiman's famous quote, "You can do anything, make anything, dream anything. If you can change the world, the world will change."

It gives me immense pleasure to be able to work with this consummate artist, whom I've looked up to in my formative years. We've successfully been able to fuse in the idea of Art and Production Science by combining Glenn's unmatched art practice and my company's deep knowledge of production, making art pieces accessible to the world. Very few artists have been able to transcend the boundaries of art and understand the value of reaching out to bigger audience by going commercial. Glenn and I have been fortunate to have mastered this process.

The teacher in Glenn is very successfully able to break down his artistry into small and logical steps that our team dedicated to Glenn's project capably interprets and transmutes into reality. He has a very precise (over 30 steps) cutting process of a single piece. He makes light dance on gemstones and combines colors of two or more gemstones like no other artist does. Glenn's fluid, dynamic art transforms natural hard gem minerals into moving, melting or flying images of color and light. Each carving is one of a kind - recognized the world over as a distinctive Lehrer brand. Call this Production Science or making Accessible Art, this took a good two years and countless trips to arrive to the level where we have successfully touched lives.

Since Glenn had an 'Indian experience' early on in his life, he connects socially and spiritually very well to the people here. With this another great advantage, Glenn has leveraged a very successful East and West collaboration. We've sold over 60,000 pieces under this collaboration already and with Gemporia coming to India, we now have a platform to take our creativity to the next level. Making this beautiful art accessible to the world is what drives us and that is just what we both thrive on!

I continue to develop unique and exciting co-creative works with others in the industry. I feel my art is just beginning to take on a whole new level of creativity and beauty par excellence. The future is ripe with dreams and visions not yet imagined.

13

YOU CAN SERVE ONLY ONE OF TWO FATHERS

· Live On The Oprah Winfrey Show

"Hell is in the here and now. So is heaven. Quit worrying about the hell or dreaming about heaven, as they are both present inside this very moment. Every time we fall in love, we ascend to heaven. Every time we hate, envy, or fight someone, we tumble straight into the fires of hell."
Elif Shafak from the book "The Forty Rules of Love" (pg 182)

This is the hardest chapter I've had to write. It is one of those stories I struggled to decide whether to write or not and add it into the book. This story I'm about to tell may irk some individuals and their religious belief systems. So, whatever your religious background or belief systems are, I ask that you suspend your judgment about what you believe are or think, and be open to what you're about to read. Please just hear me out with an open mind.

The year was 1989 and Shirley MacLaine and "The New

Age" was just placed on the cover of Time Magazine. Somehow this was to be the ultimate of the dawning of the Age of Aquarius - or something of that order - now having gone mainstream since it was on the cover of a national news magazine like Time. Crystals and Crystal Energy was somehow now in everyone's consciousness. What I had experienced back in 1972, The New Age, was now somehow part of the mainstream of American culture, having come of age in 1989. All of sudden it seemed as though everyone was getting in on the act.

A good friend of mine at the time, Marilyn Ferguson, who wrote the New Age classic book, "The Aquarian Conspiracy", was asked to be on the Oprah Winfrey show to come on and talk about this New Age phenomenon going mainstream. Apparently, the producers of Oprah's show were putting together a panel of 5 to be representatives of different aspects of the New Age. One of the panelists they were looking for was an expert in the Crystal Energy field, to come on and discuss this new rage called, Crystal Power. My name was given to them by Marilyn as someone whom they should interview for the show considering my background in both metaphysics and gemology.

I received a phone call from a producer of the show who interviewed me to find out if I would be this person. They asked several questions of me as to what I would be saying on live TV. It was all very exciting. I felt that what I had been experiencing and teaching since 1976 had finally gone mainstream. Crystals and their metaphysics had now gone mainstream and was going to be broadcasted nationwide in the USA. Apparently, I was this perfect person to be the panelist on Crystals. At the time, I felt my time had come and I could share with clarity my experiences and knowledge to the public, hoping to clarify and take some of the "woo woo" out of what so many in the metaphysical community were professing. I really wanted to give sound science along with my spiritual experiences as a way for individuals to understand what the commotion was all about, without it being disregarded as some healy feely crazy as so many were being labeled as at the time. Somewhat of a derogatory term, "healy feely" is used by the mineral and gem industry to describe individuals who got into minerals for the energy and metaphysics.

I was thrilled they picked me to appear on national TV. This would be my very first live TV experience and with Oprah Winfrey, whom I had heard was really into crystals and metaphysics. And the producers mention, "Oh yes, Oprah loves crystals, so please if you can bring some of your crystals with you to the show for display that would be great." The panel of "experts" were my friend Marilyn, a "Norman Vincent Peel" white suit dressed Unity church minster from Texas, Kevin Ryerson, one of today's best-known New Age channelers, myself and one New Age debunker to counter this new cultural phenomena.

When I entered the studio set I was shown where I would be sitting and where I could set up a small display for my crystals. Before the show started, Oprah came over to introduce herself to me and to admire my crystals. She was really enjoying them and one in particular was speaking to her. She then said how after the show she would love to talk to me about this one crystal I had on display. I'm thinking how great it would be if Oprah got one of my stones. This would be such a wonderful thing.

The show started out with each of the panelists sharing five minutes of expertize. I remember talking about how molecules bond in an intelligent manner to create these beautiful symmetrical forms. This in itself was energy and the planet Earth's intelligences. When individuals touch, feel and interact with crystals they are tuning into the cosmic intelligence of our universe. This is undeniable. Plus, Quartz crystal's ability to modulate and focus energy known as "piezoelectric" was the one advent that has brought about the 20th century Age of Information. We would not have radios, computers or telephone communication without this scientific attribute. Quartz crystals was all about communication. So, to understand this one could tune into them as an energy modulator of one's thoughts and feelings as a perfect tool for consciousness.

At this point I was feeling really good that I had done a decent job in communicating the unseen world of metaphysics with the seen world of physics. Once each of the panelists had a chance to say what they had to about this New Age phenomenon, Oprah then turned to the audience for a question and answer session.

The very first person whom she picked ended up setting the tone for the rest of the show.

This woman in the audience stands up and says, "We can only serve one of two Fathers. Our Father Lord in Heaven or the Father the Devil". It was not a question but a statement. At this moment I'm thinking, "Where is this all going to lead?" I could not believe that Oprah was taking this conversation in this direction. Clearly this woman was accusing us of serving the Devil and not her view of who God was to her, in her faith.

First the Unity Minster Kevin Ryerson spoke from a biblical stand point about what this woman just stated. I knew full well one cannot win in a conversation like this, because beliefs like this woman's are locked into the dogma of her religious beliefs. I have no problem with individual's beliefs and convictions from a religious standpoint. I come from, "To each their own". In my mind, every religion points to the same direction: a belief in God and devotion. This is beautiful, all religions lead to the same source. What I do have problem is that often dogma leaves no open door for a conversation for others to have a faith or belief in a different path of devotion. To me religion and one's spirituality is their own and who am I to judge which path is the right one. It is for each person to decide this for themselves. It is not me or anyone else to right to judge another in their faith and devotion. It is and always will be a personal choice that is no one else's. This conversation on TV was a closed, no win situation.

All too often I've come to believe that one loses touch with their own spirituality when they turn to religious dogma that tells them how to be devout, how to live and how to pray. I've seen it my own heritage of Judaism, in Christianity as well as Hinduism and Buddhism. I've learned to respect every religion because it is just another face of God. All religions lead us to the same place. Our direct connection to God, Goddess, All There Is (Lazaris). Faith is a very personal and unique path for each and every one of us. No religion is better than another, all lead to the one God Source. More importantly, it's how one's heart and mind connect that is the real true path. All lead to the same source, known as God Consciousness, solely based on my own personal experiences, my travels around the world and my personal studies of the bible, the Qur'an and Hindu Scriptures. How can one's God be any better than anyone else's? We all come from the same source and return to the same source.

When the Unity Minster and Kevin Ryerson finished trying to answer the woman from an evaluated Christian stand point, I felt compelled to say something. I started out by acknowledging that the person in the audience was absolutely correct in her statement. One can only serve one of two Fathers. This I came to know through my experience and studies with my Sufi teacher as well as my own cosmic out of body experiences.

So, I started out by saying, "Madam, you're absolutely correct in this statement. But let me give a modern "New Age" interpretation of what the Bible has been saying for centuries. One is either coming from a God of Love in their heart, or coming from Fear and Hate in one's heart. These are the two Fathers one has to choose in his or her own heart daily."

Thinking this was a good answer and we can now move on and really begin to discuss   questions about the New Age, instead everything went downhill from here. The next individual Oprah picks was exactly the same as the first. The audience had been stuffed with Born Again Christians who believed their faith is the only way. Again, I don't have an issue with individuals who have discovered Jesus as their Lord and Savior, for He was all about Love. This much I have learned reading the New Testament. He was an amazing Being who truly had been chosen by God to share his wisdom, love and miracles so others could find their way out of darkness and into the light. For the period Jesus walked this earth, there was much darkness in his world at that time. Jesus is the way for some, but from my experiences and wisdom by this time, he for sure is not the only way and I know this runs counter with those whom believe Jesus being the only way.

So, it appears the producers of the Oprah Winfrey show had stuffed the audience with many devout Christians just to create a shock TV reality show. I get it, but this was so counter to being able to really share what the New Age is about and not about. After three or four in the audience all spouting the same dogma I realized this was going nowhere, so I just shut my mouth, crossed my arms and sat in silence on TV for the next 45 minutes, fully aware that it would matter little what I or any of us on this panel can really speak of the New Age without being cut down by a one-way narrow view of God and Life.

Towards the end of the show Oprah has a caller call in to ask a question. This male voice comes on, sounding very sad and despondent. He begins by saying that, "I am an alcoholic, I lost my job and my wife has left me. My life is mess and how can the New Age help me." All the panelists were completely silent to this caller's question, not sure how to answer him. I felt I had to speak up and say, "You first need to get in touch with your feelings. It all starts there". I'm about to finish what I'm about to say but Oprah quickly interrupts me and says, "That's easy for you to say." And before I have a chance to respond she then cuts me off and says, "We have to end it here and take a station break for commercials". I am furious at this, as I could not finish what I was going to say. If she had just given me another 30 seconds I was going to answer, "I am fully aware what you must be going through. I grew up in an alcoholic family. Though my Dad was a hardworking and enterprising man, he did have a drinking problem until he became completely sober at the age of 53. The one thing missing while I was growing up was that no one in my family was honest about their feelings." Change always begins when one first, comes to the truth about what one is really feeling and why one turns to something like alcohol to numb the pain. I will inject here that when my father did go sober for the next 39 years, we were able to come back together, deepen our relationship and come to a more loving place towards the end of his life".

I found myself so incensed by the whole experience on the Oprah show, as soon as the show ended I packed my crystals and just walked out of the studio and did not wait to even talk to Oprah about the crystal she was interested in.

I was so angry by the fact that they had not really wanted to discuss what the real meaning of the New Age was, instead they turned the whole experience into some circus show for the shock factor. There was no substance, just this type of shock reality TV. I felt I was lied to by the producers when I was first interviewed over the phone and seduced to come on and be ridiculed. I walked out of that studio and did not look back.

After the TV program, I wondered what difference did my presence matter. I didn't really say that much. I don't think anybody heard me or understood me…

The next day when I returned home, my mother-in-law, Mildred Jeffrey, called me to congratulate me. The first thing I said to Millie was, "How can you say that? There was really nothing truly said just this shock TV scenario where they placed dozens of Fundamental Christians to mock us and discredit us. It was a circus for TV ratings."

The next thing Millie said absolutely blew me away. "Glenn, never underestimate your impact. Remember you were looking at maybe a hundred or so who were in the audience live on the show. Don't forget the millions of TV viewers who were watching this show across America. That was the real audience and they could see the truth. What you had to say was powerful. You were really good and know that it did have an effect for those watching."

I realized I had not even thought of this. Millie was absolutely correct. I was focused and thinking of only the audience in front of me and not that I was being watched across America. All those millions of viewers that tuned in who maybe could see through the circus charade and hear the grain of truth each of us was sharing on the panel.

I want to personally share a bit about my mother-in-law Millie, in that she was not your ordinary run of the mill mother-in-laws. So was a powerhouse of a women. Although she was the stereotypical character when Sharon and I first got together. She did everything she could to try and make it not happen with her daughter marring me. I did not have a college degree; big minus. I was this hippie artist; another minus. On paper, I did not stand up to her standards. But eventually I won her over with Love and Sharon would say, "She got to know my core and my substance. Then I was her shining son-in-law."

Standing at 4'10", weighing less than 100 lbs. Millie was a living legend in her own right. From the 1950s onward, Mildred Jeffery was a major mover and shaker of American politics. She was the highest-ranking women in the United Auto Workers union. She worked closely and held the ear of both President JF. Kennedy and his brother Robert Kennedy when it came to labor, civil and women's rights. She served as President of the Board of Governors for Wayne State University and received the Medal of Freedom from then President Bill Clinton. The medal of Freedom is the highest honor an American non-military citizen can receive from a seated president. She was awarded it for her decades of work for unions, women's rights, and minority rights, and had the ears of seated presidents and presidential candidates. Millie was a power-house and not someone to go up against her unless you had your facts in order. So, for Millie to call me and tell me the impact I had on National TV was no small act.

She was instrumental in awakening me to the impact one can have in society and culture. Each one of us has impact and our acts do matter. I keep this in mind every time I go live on national TV.

A couple days later, I'm back in San Francisco riding in an elevator in a hotel when a man in the elevator turns to me and say, "I know you from somewhere". I'm great with remembering faces, but I look at him and realize I've never seen this person before. I then say, "I don't think so. I'm great with faces and I don't recognize you." Then what came out of his mouth was a surprise. He said, "Yes, now I know where I've seen you. You were on the Oprah Winfrey show the other day. You were fantastic." I'm thinking, really? I turn to him and say, "The show was a joke with how they played us by stuffing the audience with Born Again Christians, calling us the Devil and worshiping with crystals and the New Age."

What he said next really was another surprise. "What you had to say was good, but what you did not say by just sitting there for most of the hour had a tremendous impact. The fact that you just sat there with crossed arms and remained silent and did not fall into the trap by engaging the audience in a no-win conversation had such a powerful impact. Your quiet presence said more than any words could say. You were great on the show."

Wow, another person helping me to realize how powerful just one's presence can have on others. The moral of this story is never underestimate your impact. We all have effect on our reality with our very thought and feeling, whether spoken or merely thought in mind and heart. They go out into the world like ripples on a pond. My presence on the stage and the very the few things I said, but in fact the majority of what I did not say had maybe a meaning and impact to all those millions of people watching the show nationwide.

What I gleaned from this experience is: Never underestimate when your presence, and the few or many words you speak, may touch another; this you can't predict. There were probably many others who were watching this show who had similar reactions as Millie and the stranger. I now realized I had been a positive influence. I now know it's more important what my intention or my motivation is when I do speak. At that moment on TV I knew that I didn't want to further flame the fires of conflict... I didn't want to participate in the conversation knowing full well it would only perpetuate the polarity that the show was trying to create. I now realize that sometimes silence can be the best communicator.

The old Lao Tzu Proverb rings true here, "He who knows, does not say. He who says often does not know". Now that I've appeared live several times a year on Gemporia TV, my presence, my knowledge and the beauty I share with as much conscious intent as I can I know it can have major impact. So many have written to me to confirm this fact. The fact that the creation of my beautiful work has major personal impact on so many others. And the knowledge I share is an inspiration to so many in filling in a richness to the beauty in my jewelry.

14

TRANSFORMATIONAL CRYSTALLOGRAPHY

· Grounded in Modern Mineralogy
· Gemstones and Big History as We Know It

"Before there is creation, there is geometry."
Plato

"Before there is geometry there is light."
Glenn Lehrer

"The ultimate goal is to regain the whole by knowing how the parts fit together."
Arthur Young

"...Joy and amazement at the beauty and grandeur of this world of which man can just form a faint notion..."
Albert Einstein

At this juncture in my life, all these individual parts of my quest have come together in this almost molecular, co-creative relationship, to where my life, knowledge, wisdom and art flow seamlessly in and out of one another. I feel as though an alchemical process has occurred within me and I'm conscious of the fact. It is the sum total of the parts of who I am that have melded into a profound, living, breathing experience of living life to its fullest. I feel I have achieved a unique understanding paired with a personal wisdom of my conscious self in relationships with myself, others and with Nature herself. I sense I have opened a window to some grander, brilliant continuum about life and the nature of consciousness. Increasingly aware the observer and the participant are one in the quantum of life. Becoming more conscious on a daily basis I have impact in my world by either creating or allowing within my reality (Lazaris).

This is the final chapter in this journey of a lifetime where I've shared with you some of my more intimate, deeper true stories that have had major impact in my life. Extraordinary experiences: travels to far corners of the Earth coupled with a lifetime of gemology, gem cutting and a personal spiritual pursuit. What was revealed to me so many years ago in the out-of-body experience to the core of the atom and the subsequent years of spiritual pursuit, I have developed a tool whereby we as individuals can reflect and contemplate how we individually structure our thoughts and feelings metaphorically to one of the crystal structures as defined in the Seven Crystal Systems of Mineralogy.

Starting way back in 1972, at that moment I was taken to the core of an atom in that raptured state of awareness, to then discovering the connection between the physical and metaphysical when I learned the language of science in my mineralogy courses, I was now able to communicate this grand understanding with a language. The language of science was to me the best way to explain this most indescribable mystical state. One could metaphorically say my two halves met and were woken up. Just like in quantum physics, "Is it the particle or is it the wave? Are we observing or participating in life?" There are many ways to say the same point: my Adam meets my Eve, my Masculine meets my Feminine, the Electron is bonded to the Proton. So much so that this cosmic dance of the understanding of science, blended with my visions beyond this physical dimension, coupled with unbridled exploration for my art, I feel I have found this deeper inner unity and harmony. Life is not perfect but as a conscious person I now realize how connected every particle is to one another in the known universe. We are in the end part of a continuum in this evolution of life whereby we are constantly observing and participating in life at every instant. The ancient Greek word "Krystallos" means crystal, but can also been heard as "Krysto" which means Christ the Illuminated One. So similar is the derivation of these two ancient Greek words in that they illuminate light out into the world. The very principles of a natural mineral crystal, just by being itself, can be seen as a map that represents in symmetry, transparency and brilliance the very act and state of being, that we as humans live and dream by. We are one: every particle is talking to every particle throughout our known universe.

In this chapter I will share a theory of what was borne that night I was taken to the core of the atom. How this Being of Light, so many years ago, in that out-of-body, transcendental state showed me the very physics that makes up our known physical world of atoms and elements. The very stuff of our known universe can transcend the physical properties of matter and lift one's understanding to a place of self-realization. It was at this transcendental moment I came to experience the power of resonance and how the physical world is the final stage of manifestation. Resonances that set the stage for all patterns to form from light to matter.

After my own personal insight into this Big History, I will formulate a much-abridged version of crystallography, to start you off on the part of science that is so embedded in my life and philosophy.

Big History: From the Core of the Atom to the Pinnacle of Consciousness

This repeating pattern of atoms bonding three-dimensionally into molecules (as seen in gemstones on our planet) become highly refractive, transparent objects, frozen in geological time in this end state. I have come to theorize that minerals and gemstones are the first idealized forms of matter on our planet, and they represent great sentinels of the Book of Life – representing where we are at the zenith of this continuum. I like to use gemstones metaphorically as archetypes as to how we structure our lives personally, socially and as a race of conscious beings, emerging from this continuum of inorganic and organic life, to currently reach this amazing pinnacle of consciousness itself: Human Beings.

There are eight thresholds of transformation as laid out by David Christian that set the stage for Earth to form and transform from energy into more and more complex systems. This is where Big History took macro steps to becoming complex organic and inorganic forms of energy and life. I've included this to give you a greater sense of the magnitude of change that had to have occurred just to set the stage for the Earth to form, and for minerals and gemstones to be created on our planet, let alone how we as humans have evolved out of this cosmic soup.

At this moment in Deep Time we now are witnessing simplicity moving to complexity. We are living in the springtime of this movement from simple to complex in the great cycle of order to disorder and bonding again in order. The ever-evolving steps of evolution of life and the known universe.

The threshold moments (or portal transition) for our universe to exist as we know is given below in geological time. This is known as "The Big History".

1. The Big Bang 14.5 Billion Years Ago
From a point of singularity emerges a mega explosion that gives birth to our known Universe.

2. Stars Light Up in a Cooling Universe
Hydrogen and Helium begin to condense at 10,000,000° Celsius, and atoms begin to appear. The building blocks have been laid as the foundation of elemental complexity.

3. Complex Elements
Complex elements begin their formation. Each star becomes an element factory. From this point the universe and its building blocks are laid. What is so fascinating is it takes at least two more star collisions to occur to get to the level where enough of the elements are created for life even to begin to exist. It is with each subsequent explosion that enough energy is released to create more and more complex elements of protons and electrons. To where enough is created as seen

through the Periodical Table of Elements at complexity of form that can begin its process of build first inorganic forms (the pinnacle being minerals and gemstones) then more and more complex bio life to emerge.

4. Earth Forms – 4.5 Billion Years Ago

A series of collisions with other objects in space bring water and rare elements to Earth. Then a Moon is created via another collision with another planet creating a balance in Earth's rotation, preparing for balanced seasons to occur.

5. The Origin of Life Forms

This begins the Human Factor - 542 million years ago. Seas explode with life of many different forms. All of a sudden complex life emerges. A unique principle to this is the more complex the life form, the more vulnerable that life is to mega changes.

6. Collective Learning

Database of knowledge is built. Hunting and gathering in early human development.

7. The Farming Revolution

The Empire of Man. Ten thousand years ago, farming helps us become the masters of our world. Natural World becomes our laboratory. Division of labor begins. Empires emerge. Language is developed via writing, knowledge passes from generation to generation.

8. The Modern Revolution

The great accelerator: information. The Human Factor now dominates the bio-sphere. Now every two years our collective knowledge is doubling.

The very DNA of life from the atom to the molecule, organic or inorganic are building blocks of complexity, symmetry and order, ever-evolving in new formations that continue to reflect the very beauty that shone from the very first burst of light that emanated for the Big Bang. "Let there be Light".

Deep within the core of the Earth is a fiery, molten, chaotic soup of cosmic particles, always continually generating and moving as outward tension in the Earth's timeless motion. Beyond the Earth itself lies the great, cold void of space, composed of many forms of radiant energy, swirling in every direction, creating constant compression on our small, seemingly defenseless planet.

The necessary protective phenomenon which occurs between these two tremendously opposing forces is the Earth's crust. Calling it the crossover area, it is the formation of a scab-like skin which coats and contains the roiling alchemist's cauldron of the Earth's core. This crust is the zone of equalization where the external compression of space meets with the internal expansion of tension. It is here in a portion of the Earth's crust where the ideal conditions exist for crystals to take birth and grow, in the ever slowly cooling and compressing chambers.

At a certain stage of cooling and condensing these particles began forming sub-atomic and atomic particles i.e. protons, neutrons, and electrons. These atomic particles then began arranging themselves in numerous numerical arrangements to form elements. These elements either combined with themselves or with other types of elements to now form a molecule. Molecules are the basic seed from which a crystal can now take form. A crystal is an orderly arrangement of atoms in a 360 degree lattice network or structure. Ninety nine percent of all minerals in the mineral kingdom are crystals. Pure Quartz crystal is only one type, though its basic molecular structure of silicon and oxygen comprise about 25% of the known minerals.

With a few exceptions to the rule, all igneous-forming minerals are silicates, constituting well over 90% of the Earth's crust. The eight most common elements in nature are oxygen with 62.5%, silica with 21.2%, aluminum with 6.5%. Then iron, magnesium, calcium, sodium, and potassium taking up the balance of 9.8% in varying degrees of concentration.

Before I dive into Transformational Crystallography I want first to paint a picture in words of a short brief story as to what it takes for a gemstone to form on a planet. For a mineral to even get to a point where a gemstone can begin to form, a planet in this vast universe needs to go through several major cataclysmic transformations of meteorite strikes, vast magma volcanic chemical events to unfold and for tectonic plates of land to move. Every catastrophic impact on Earth is like a huge mineral factory creating new forms with every major change. A magnitude of force beyond what our small (in comparison) mental minds can simply comprehend. A magnitude of such great force that it melts, mixes and cools just right for a gemstone to form in a vast land mass of rock. I like to term it as Mother Nature's oven where she bakes her gems. Imagine gemstones as fruits of the tree in the inorganic world of minerals. The end results of transformative changes in the Earth's evolution on the mineral world. In all, Earth's crust occupies less than 1% of Earth's volume and it is only within this thin section where minerals and gemstones form.

As the individual, in consciousness, we walk upon this Earth. Our feet are on the ground and our heads are in the sky. We stand between these two great forces of tension and compression. It is here on the far outer skin of the Earth's crust that we gather information and construct it into knowledge. Reflecting on the Axis of Symmetry to your life just may give you clues to insights to your life.

It was in the mineral kingdom that we first began our comprehension of space with form, where pure mathematics of consciousness could be stored. A reference library, a road map to the direction of the way back home. Stored in our individual and collective consciousness are many road signs called archetypal symbols. They stand like tall ancient monoliths, crossing cultural and social boundaries. An archetypal symbol can be defined as an original model, the first mold from which many models were built after. These archetypal symbols become pockets of stored information, much like a database in computers; the original grid work of any subsequent programs that are written. An archetypal symbol is an image that carries a condensed amount of information that has maintained itself over a long period of time to emerge as data accessible by anyone on the planet, manifesting itself in similarities throughout various cultures. The mineral kingdom and the geometry of the crystal systems can be seen as these ancient pockets of divine knowledge. Externally, crystals appear to be too perfect to have formed naturally, as though we had some doing in their shape. Internally, hidden deep in their microcosm world is the very code in which the DNA of life has taken its very blueprint. The wonder and magic of the mineral kingdom and its unfolding symmetry can become one of our best road maps to contemplating the questions of, "Who am I?", "Where have

I come from?", and "Where is it that I am going?"

I am excited to share my Theory of Transformational Crystallography, as it is reflected through our thoughts and feelings, choices and decisions, coupled with the way we structure our lives, relationships and culture on a larger scale. The geometry and symmetry is uncanny from the mineral to human world. How the very axis of symmetry seen in nature is a mirror in how we formulate and define our world around us, each individually. How the world of natural crystallography is a mirror and archetype to much in the way we as humans begin to structure our lives and environments. The blue print is so natural.

I will share with you my theory of a present day, modern, natural Earth-based tool for personal self-reflection. Similar to astrology in the way it may give an individual a clue about oneself, this form of an oracle is completely Earth-based. It is being defined by my exploration and combined experiences using modern mineralogy's definition of the Seven Crystal Systems and how we as humans structure our thoughts and feelings, our relationships and society on a much larger scale.

The Seven Crystal Systems in Mineralogy are based upon an axis of symmetry where there is a north, south, east, west, an above and below orientation - the same way we define crystal symmetry.

I am asking you to take a giant leap here with me if you are skeptical about what I'm about to present. The Seven Crystal Systems of Mineralogy in Nature can be seen metaphorically as a map to our thinking, feeling, being and actions we undertake in life. The geometry on this physical plane is a long evolution from the mineral, to the plant, to the animal culminating to us as humans. The atoms are the same, just more complex and more diverse. Call it evolution. The paradox is: 'We Are All One' but infinitely diverse.

I have tested Transformational Crystallography on hundreds of individuals over the last 39 years and it has been uncannily accurate in what it can tell us as individuals about how we structure our thoughts and feelings and why individually we make certain choices and decisions. Each mineral crystal has a defined symmetry of structure.

Though one cannot see this structure physically per se in one's thoughts and feelings, we all have defined our lives by length, breadth and depth. This geometry that is reflected in gemstones remains a pattern in which we as humans use as a blue print unwittingly throughout our lives to give us meaning and dimension.

Before I venture further in this chapter I would like to address the "New Age" emergence in the late 20th century of what has been termed, "crystal power or energy". Though what I have to say is not the final or definitive, there are a few elements I feel I need to define from my experience and knowledge of studying and working with these very rare gemstones for many years.

The term Power is almost a misnomer as it applies to crystals. The definition for the word Power, is the ability to act, pure and simple. Crystals, then, do not fit this term since from a physical stand point they can't act. I like to say they just "Be". But this very "Being" in a crystal holds resonance because of its defined symmetry of the way atoms have bonded in a highly symmetrical, repeating 3D structure. It holds an intelligence seen on the atomic level and reflected by its outer crystal form.

Now, the word "energy" can be applied with the scientific principle of piezoelectric which is found in many minerals in various degrees. Quartz and Tourmaline are two gemstone minerals that exhibit this natural ability. The simple layman explanation for piezoelectric is: if you strike a mechanical blow to one of these minerals, the mineral will give off an electrical current. Electrons jump out of their orbit. And inversely if you deliver an electrical current to a mineral with this ability, it will mechanically expand and contract like a heartbeat. A great example of this modern phenomenon is the Quartz movement wrist watch. With a battery that sends an electrical current into a Quartz crystal wafer, the Quartz wafer will expand and contract, thus moving the watch movement parts to tick away seconds, minutes, hours and days. Drawing from this physical property and connecting it on a metaphysical and Quantum mechanics level, your thoughts and feelings give out and receive information every moment of your breathing awake or dreaming state. Do they have impact and power? Yes, they do. Can you draw a straight line? Not always, but it's called living one's life for positive or negative ends, meaning one is constantly having impact in one's life. One only needs to contemplate this to know this is true. No matter what, the strong attraction for human nature to be near and to be adorned with gemstones is ancient and as old as our known civilization on this planet. The mystery lies in this very fact.

The Seven Crystal Systems for all known minerals is the language developed back in the mid-1800s by minerologist

James Dana to classify the differences using geometric coordinates for each, based on an Axis of Symmetry. In non-mathematical terms, think of these axes' directions as a north and south pole, an east and west direction, and an above and below axis. These three imaginary axes with their corresponding directions all intersect one another either at a 90 degree, 30/60 degree, or obtuse and acute angles to one another. Length, width and breadth take on seven unique relationship of the axis and how they intersect with one another. In the case of two of the Systems there are four axes instead of three.

I make a bold leap here by correlating the parallel between mineral crystals and how we as humans structure our thoughts and feelings, our interpersonal relationships and society on a much larger scale; physically, mentally and emotionally. Think of these six or eight coordinates as what's in front of you as your future; behind you is the past; to the left is your receptive nature; to the right as your dynamic nature; above is how you connect to All There Is; and below is how all becomes grounded in one's own world.

These three or four axes involve themselves within one's heart and mind, thoughts and feelings, giving your life meaning and ultimately dimension. I am suggesting here, we are reflecting in some mystical way the very archetypal patterns laid down at the early birth of our Universe when plasma began to form solids, and terrestrial earths were being formed. They can be seen as blueprints or archetypes to our own evolutionary process. In crystals, it is called the unit cell: the simplest combining of elements into a molecule that lays down the blue print for that crystal to grow repetitively.

Before I get into the substance of my theory I want to lay a bit of ground work and give you a small sense of the magnitude that our universe has to go through before minerals can even form. Life as we know it is a complex blending and recombining of the available chemistry, powered by the physics of the birth of our universe after the Big Bang. From the very core of an atom, through all living life forms, all the way to human self-consciousness, life as we know it is an ever-changing, evolving repeating cycle from chaos to singularity and often back into chaos. The very formation of the elements created in that moment of the Big Bang become the very atoms our body is composed of. We are made up of the very stuff that was created at the birth of our universe 14.5 billion years ago. It has just evolved, been broken down and remade over and over again until it has evolved the life on our planet. We as humans are the tip of this spear of a long evolution of formation, dissolution and reformation as the very stuff of the universe constantly evolves. This stuff that the universe is made up of appears to be constantly ever striving for greater and greater levels of complexity and consciousness. This seems to be at the core of every pulse of an atom to every breath of life. It's in all of us and everything around us in this vast universe.

Life is always seeking the most stable state of harmony and balance as it is ever-evolving and expanding in greater and greater combination of complexity and function. It is in the mineral kingdom where one can see Nature seeking her highest state of symmetry and perfection through the organization of atoms based on the laws of resonance. This very law that governs atoms create the very drive to seek the most stable state of perfection. This idealized state is what we've called as suspended animation, or from a scientific definition, minus 273 degrees kelvin. This state of perfection can never be achieved, but it is the very drive that moves all life in the forward movement to the future and to find a bond in relationship that is strong and stable. From a human vantage point we call it Harmony and Peace of Mind. Gemstones and natural minerals are a high order on the atomic level in Earth's complexity in an inorganic state. Complex in its combination of elements that form a repeating pattern of symmetry to become this absolutely transparent highly refractive substance. This amazing piece of knowledge that reflects an alchemy is a brilliant insight to the complex order of the Earth's intelligence.

Throughout human history metaphysicians and mystics have been saying that all life, animate and inanimate is seeking that idealized state called perfection or union with the One. From chaos, all forms of life seek the most stable state of balance and harmony. Out of cosmic disorder the universe is seeking harmony with the rhythms and patterns of the universe that are in constant motion. This one principle of harmony drives every form from atoms to crystals to humans. It is the inner drive to achieve the most stable state of idealized perfection that drives us as humans to achieve our very best in life. Minerals are a reflection in life that show us that through chaos one can seek a state of elegance where the light of one's souls and spirit can shine and inspires other to feel inspired. Some have called them saints or messiahs. I'll leave that up to the theologians to define.

This ideal state is never reached by the universe, but is ever-expanding and defining new boundaries of harmony with greater levels of complexity and diversity. Of course, chaos is always around the corner, ready to destroy, yet again only to build new atoms, new forms, new galaxies. Maybe even new gemstones to come along and be discovered in this day and age. Reflected throughout human culture and history, one can see these very principles emulating Nature's drive towards perfection in our history and civilizations of humanity through its architecture, arts and science. Evolution is always reaching for more or better. Nature's compulsive drive towards this idealized state called perfection.

Transformational Crystallography™: The Seven Crystal Systems of Consciousness in Nature™ and The Geometry and Color of Consciousness

Transformational Crystallography is a powerful key and a tool to inner consciousness. A revolutionary link between one's mystical origins and the physical universe. It is an oracle and spiritual tool for the 21st century. Transformational Crystallography, the Seven Crystal Systems of Consciousness in Nature™ is a seven-step process that mirrors our very own consciousness seeking harmony and balance in all aspects of our lives and spiritual evolution. The Seven Crystal Systems is based on the science of crystallography as defined by modern day mineralogy and Transformational Crystallography, a revolutionary spiritual tool that can link one's consciousness to the laws of resonance and manifestation. It can also serve as a powerful catalyst to explore beyond one's waking conscious mind and how it sets boundaries and define one's space in function and substance in all levels of life.

Transformational Crystallography was revealed to me in that out of body mystical state over four decades ago. It has been a spiritual journey and personal discovery over these past 40 years to continue to explore and test Transformational

Crystallography. It is what moved me to be a Gem Artist and gemologist. Through years of spiritual work and personal mystical experiences, along with introducing, teaching and experimenting with several hundred individuals, this personal diagnostic tool continues to be uncanny in what it can bring into focus in one's life. Transformational Crystallography is a genuine oracle to one's most inner being as a conscious thinking and feeling person, deeply ground in the very chemistry and physics of our sacred planet Earth and the mysteries of us as conscious human forms on this planet. It is an archetypal link between our knowledge of science and our own personal spiritual heritage that is this long journey for the soul be at home with "All There Is." (Lazaris)

There are over 4,000-plus known minerals found in nature and almost every one has a unique, repeating crystal structure and axis of symmetry. Quartz - often referred to as crystal - is only one type of crystal and defined by only one of the seven crystal systems that is used to classify minerals according to their defined symmetry. One hundred and seventy nine years ago, Dana first published and defined in science the symmetry of crystallization in the mineral field. Dana was the first person to classify minerals into an arrangement by composition and structure. In other words, by its chemistry and its geometric symmetry that each mineral's habit exhibited. However, this system did not arise spontaneously, but developed over a long period of time over eight editions. The first five editions of A System of Mineralogy, were published in 1837, 1844, 1850, 1854, and 1868, and were authored or revised by James Dwight Dana. In the field of mineralogy and gemology this system is a molecular system definition for each mineral in nature.

Symmetry is defined in Dana's Textbook of Mineralogy 4th ed. by W.E. Ford, "The faces of a crystal are arranged according to certain laws of symmetry, and this symmetry is the natural basis of the division of crystals into systems and classes." There are three types of symmetry as one views the crystal structure and corresponding system, (1) a plane of symmetry, (2) an axis of symmetry and (3) a center of symmetry.

A crystal system is based on the axis of symmetry (imaginary lines running through the crystal interior from either face to face, point to point, or edge to edge). Whilst the outer shape/form of the crystal that you can see with the naked eye is the crystal habit. When standing up, run a line from top of your head to your feet and that is your vertical axis (C axis), from which all other directions are measured.

There are seven distinct crystal systems in which all minerals form from. The Seven Systems are:

1. **Triclinic**
2. **Monoclinic**
3. **Orthorhombic**
4. **Isometric**
5. **Tetragonal**
6. **Hexagonal**
7. **Trigonal**

As a way to start I would like you to turn over the next few pages and pick one of the geometric symbols shown. The seven are played out with their corresponding mineral definitive name. Then visualize a color that you are most often attracted to. Hold on to the symbol and color and then begin the article. The gemstones are of the 30 most known and use in the mineral kingdom. It does not have to stop here. There are over 4,000 different known minerals in the mineral kingdom. The article will then go on to introduce and explain the science and metaphysical principals.

Transformational Crystallography, The Seven Crystal Systems as Found in Nature and their Physical, Metaphysical and Spiritual Properties

The basic short meaning for each of the Seven Crystal Systems in the seven step process of consciousness of thinking and feeling.

1. Triclinic
Function. Purpose comes into view. Freedom without responsibility. Intuition. Genius moment. New horizon. Ideas made conscious. A healing process of change.

2. Monoclinic
Substance. Value. Emotion. Giving meaning to the function with the power of emotion.

3. Orthorhombic
Form. Intellect. Structure defined. Form defined by substance. The need to belong - to have purpose with conscious intent.

4. Isometric
Idealized state. Union. Function and form are in unison and perfect balance here. The most determined and idealized state, the fulcrum from what was to what could be. Love realized.

5. Tetragonal

Going beyond boundaries. Change and transformation. New function emerging from the need to change from older forms to something new and expanded. New understandings, pushing for a deeper meaning. Reach for a greater purpose.

6. Hexagonal

Elevated new substance. New complexity. Deeper knowing and complexity of function in its substance. Elevated emotions and meaning. Complexity with diversity.

7. Trigonal

Elevated new function. Freedom with responsibility. Transcendence. Elevated intuition. Achieving a new tier of knowing and understanding. Feeling as though living one's destiny. Self realization. Enlightenment with a dynamic state of actualization.

The crystal systems start out with the least amount of symmetry, moving to the Isometric which is the most perfect balanced form. Then the urge to transcend beyond this balanced static state to seeking to new function, substance and form. See it as a whole process where there are seven distinct steps in quest for wholeness in one's life.

1. Triclinic (tri = three/clinic = angles)

Examples: Turquoise, Microcline Feldspar

Physical Properties: Three axes of unequal length, with all its intersecting lines at oblique angles. What denotes symmetry here is that the three axes intersect each other.

Metaphysical and Spiritual Properties: At point of contact all of the seven centers of the spiritual self is in disproportion to one another. Some form of great change is being called for. Native American culture has always attributed turquoise with great healing powers. Those who wear a lot of turquoise either are going through a personal healing on one or more levels of consciousness, or is a healer themselves who helps others through the process.

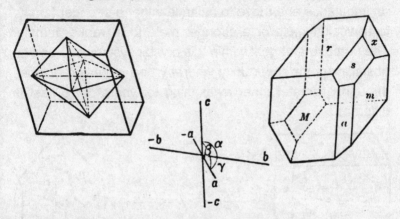

2. Monoclinic (mono=one/clinic=angle)

Examples: Jadeite, Malachite, Nephrite, Kunzite, Orthoclase

Physical Properties: Three axes of unequal lengths, two intersecting one another at right angles and the third axis intersecting them at an oblique angle.

Metaphysical and Spiritual Properties: Both the monoclinic and triclinic systems are very esoteric in that they denote a swing in the direction of a predominate force within the seven points of human consciousness in order to realign and balance an imbalanced state. For example, say your energy was most predominate on the vertical axes of awareness, your feminine/masculine was at a right angle and in balance but of shorter length and force, and your wisdom/ understanding axis was at a oblique angle to the other two axes. Now since this axis is on a incline it means that either your understanding is greater than your wisdom (appearance of arrogance) or that your wisdom is greater than your understanding (appearance of being burden). And if it was your feminine and masculine axis that is on an incline there is an imbalance and move to balance either a stronger female to a weaker male or a stronger male to a weaker female. The purpose and goal within this crystal system is to use an obstacle as an opportunity whereby one is healed or goes through a greater inner awakening to where one's past is different.

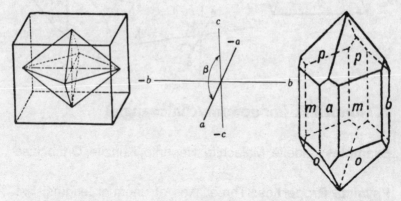

3. Orthorhombic (ortho=straight/rhombic=rectangle)

Examples: Topaz, Peridot, Chrysoberyl, and Zoisite (Tanzanite)

Physical Properties: Three crystal axes at right angles to each other all of different lengths.
Metaphysical and Spiritual Properties: The orthorhombic crystal system is similar to the tetragonal system in that

it denotes movement or change. Except where in the tetragonal you have an equal plane on the horizontal plane of consciousness here the difference in proportion to one another. My experience with this crystal system is that individuals are able to work and be with these gemstones for a much greater length of time. It can represent outer travel in parallel to inner spiritual search. Changes come in many fashions, if it was Peridot it could mean a transition though and beyond jealousy, greed and anger. If it's Topaz it could represent major motion and change in one's outer life in conjunction with new levels of inner awareness. If it's Chrysoberyl (Alexandrite & Chrysoberyl Cat's Eye) it often represents an individual who has great personal power to transform their reality. And if it was Tanzanite it can mean major breakthrough in consciousness where one goes from being in a stuck position to having received information from their higher self that completely changes their attitudes and beliefs.

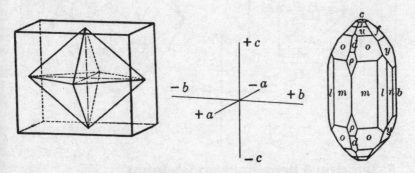

4. Isometric (iso=equal/metric=measure)

Examples: Diamond, Garnet, Fluorite

Physical Properties: Three crystal axes at right angles to each other and all of equal length.

Metaphysical & Spiritual Properties: The self in form is seen as in equal balance with the higher self and manifested self, along with equal balance between their dynamic and receptive energies, and has equal measure between their understanding and wisdom. This crystal system is seen archetypal as the self-realized individuated self. An individuated whole within a larger whole to where all one oneself is of equal balance. I have found in general that those individuals attracted to the isometric system as a primary crystalline shape are either highly individualistic or are extremely motivated in fields that require one to be in relationship of equal balance with their reality. A good example would be a mediator, arbitrator, or judge. You are either focused on the self in balance or focused on the self in balance with others.

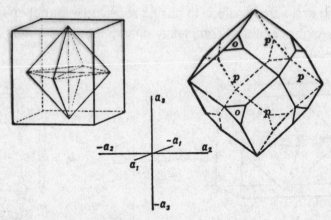

5. Tetragonal (tetra=four/gonal=form)

Example: Zircon, Scapolite

Physical Properties: Three crystal axes at right angles to each other; two of them on a horizontal plane and of equal length; the third being the vertical axis that is either longer or shorter to the other two. All three axes intersect one another at 90 degrees.

Metaphysical & Spiritual Properties: This system is where the individual is balanced equally between dynamic/receptive and understanding/wisdom. But the relationship of the vertical axes of higher and manifested self to the four horizontal components is either in greater or lesser play. Seen as a crystal system of movement either as outer travel (the shorter length) or inner travel (the longer length) the drive is for a new or elevated function in one's life. The travel is symbolic of movement that transforms oneself to greater harmonic balance. I have found that it is not a crystal system that many people would pick as a primary crystal form. It seems to be one that denotes some form of transition or change in one life at that time. Reaching for a greater sense of purpose and function from what was to what could be.

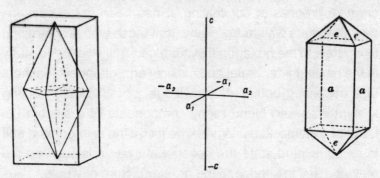

6. Hexagonal (hex=six/gonal=form) the hexagonal system

Examples: Hexagonal and Beryl (Emerald and Aquamarine)

Physical Properties: Four crystal axes, three of which are equal and lie in the horizontal plane having consistent angles

263

60 and 30 degree with each other, while the fourth axis intersects vertically at 90 degree and has a different length to the horizontal axes. Has a six-fold form of symmetry.

Metaphysical & Spiritual Properties: As the individual is channeling information between the higher self and manifested self the energy is bisected in the heart center with a clear relationship of understanding and wisdom, but the dynamic and receptive component of the self is each broken into two mirror halves. This can be viewed on different levels. One could be that within the dynamic side there is a dynamic and receptive self, thus balanced within itself. And also the receptive can be seen with both components within it. On a higher octave the dynamic self becomes an active breathing blending of understanding and wisdom and thus acts from this place. And the receptive self also becomes these generated energy of understanding and wisdom in the creative process of conceiving. It has been my experience over the years with many clients that those who are attracted to crystals in the hexagonal system generally work and study in the healing arts, visual and musical arts, channels/teachers of a contained bodies of knowledge, or individuals working to synthesis and blend many components of a system i.e. CEO of organizations. Where the isometric is seen as a self in its completed state the hexagonal system is seen as the elevated self in service to the greater picture or whole.

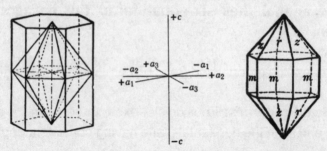

7. Trigonal or Rhombohedral

Examples: Quartz, Corundum (Ruby and Sapphire) and Tourmaline

Physical Properties: Four crystal axes, three of which are equal and lie in the horizontal plane having consistent angles 60 degrees and 30 degrees with each other, while the fourth axis intersects vertically at 90 degrees and has a different length (longer or shorter) to the horizontal axes. Having a Threefold symmetry. Representative of a new level form.

Metaphysical & Spiritual Properties: Quartz has been termed the mineral of the communication age. It has physically opened doors that were closed approximately only 100 years ago, not to mention all the attributes given to its metaphysical and spiritual doors. Where the isometric is seen as a self in its completed state, the trigonal or rhombohedral system is seen as the self-realized individual to the greater whole. The crystal system where one transcends the boundaries of the physical and becomes aware of the greater whole.

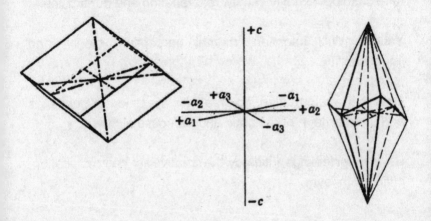

Color

To add to the complexity, color in its pure form takes the existing in the mineral kingdom to a deeper level of understanding. If you take the crystal system and add a color, one is able to grasp even a deeper level of understanding. Below is a short outline from a cross cultural perspective.

White: The color of Spirit or the All There is. White is the color in which all colors manifest out of. When white is diffracted through a prism the seven main colors appear. When you then send the seven colors back through a prism it becomes white again. Understood as the beginning and the end. If one seeks this color it can mean that their intention is to be inspired and healed by Spirit.

Red: The desire to have safety and security in one's life. Can also be seen as the explorer, adventurer, doer-dynamic, activation, manifestation.

Orange: Polarity, duality, complementary, pleasure, relationship, sexuality, family, rejuvenation and purification.

Yellow: Will, intention, mental perception, clarity, and impeccability.

Green: Transformation, co-creativity, the union of opposites and the marriage of dynamic and receptive alchemy.

Blue: Inner feelings, intimacy, the creative act, communication, giving with love.

Indigo: Perceptions, awareness, intuition, focus beyond form, inner wisdom.

Violet: Transcendence, visions, prophecy, conceiving, enlightenment, excellence, totality.

Other Colors

Pink: Divine harmony.

Mint Green: Healing.

Brown: To ground or make manifest.

Silver: The feminine or receptive energy.

Gold: The masculine or dynamic energy.

Grey: Neutral.

Black: The Void or unknown.

Transformational Crystallography: Reflecting on the Axis of Symmetry to Your Life

For the remainder of this chapter, and indeed to close the book, I will expand further on how I believe crystallography reflects our inner consciousness. This is an organic process which will allow your understanding to grow the more you open your mind and give yourself the time to absorb what I am theorizing, little by little.

I've been teaching a course in Transformational Crystallography for over 39 years to hundreds of individuals. I have come to see how gemstones and minerals are the end result of the universe's very powerful collection of forces that directs our world and binds all life to seek its highest state of perfection. They hold the very ancient archetypal principles of the universe; frozen and brilliant in our world.

Part of my theory here is that symbols matter to us, like badges, banners, uniforms, branded products, etc. They are clues and parts to our heart that connects us to the whole and helps one feel individually they matter and belong. Gemstones, the very archetype of the natural world connects us at a primordial level, much like symbols do but link us to our very DNA composed of the very stuff the Universe is made of in its evolution in the Big History of time and space. The very atoms that were created at that moment 14 billion years ago of the Big Bang is the very stuff our bodies are composed of. Whether one believes or not in the power of crystals, it does not matter because as a completely natural symbol alone it holds power on one's own body chemistry. The added power comes from knowing the immense amount of energy and change it took for this rare object to form and come into existence. Our very presence on this Earth and Her long evolution is a miracle in and of itself considering the chances, knowing what we know of how random the universe is and can be.

Let a complex system repeat itself long enough and surprises are known to happen. Simple mathematics, life and pattern. DNA holds the essence of life, printing and reprinting the pattern. Life in the universe we are now recognizing as a self-organizing repeat of a pattern as the universe continue in its expansive process.

Perfection: those moments when one feels that everything comes together. On some level it appears all life from the atom on, regarding complexity, is in quest of this perfection or heavenly state.

As an individual, in consciousness, we walk upon this Earth. Our feet are on the ground and our heads are in the sky. We stand between these two great forces of tension and compression. It is here on the far outer skin of the Earth's crust, where we are fortunately be a live on, that we gather information and construct it into knowledge. Reflecting on the Axis of Symmetry to your life, just may give you clues and insights to your life in its sense of wholeness.

Take minerals, and what is called a unit cell, defined as the simplest single unit of elements that form a unique 3D repeating pattern molecule. The unit cell defines its structure. The unit cell is the very basic combination of elements that form the molecule that becomes the pattern for repeating in a symmetrical manner. From this unit cell, along with a continuing availability of specific elements, the chemistry and the ideal conditions of the physics is what determines how big and how fine or transparent a crystal will grow in. This is seen in all of the mineral kingdom and has been classified and defined by the Seven Crystal system. Seven ways to class the way atoms stack and build using an axis of symmetry.

We used to look at life like a machine in classical physics: now you see patterning as intrinsic to life. The emerging structure of the energy seen in the shape of a Torus, such as whirlpool or hurricane. Both are water vapor or liquid moving in a spiral, an ever-flowing energy field of shape. Swirled, combined and given greater and greater complexity with each twist. This is the very pattern of life seen from the greatest galaxies to the smallest macro of an atom that is unfolding on Earth. This great pattern could be seen as the underpinning of consciousness. Awareness has its own beginning in the very self-organizing nature in the universe. What is Consciousness, or whatvare we actually looking for in this self-organizing code that continues to evolve? Call it Self-Realization or Enlightenment where in evolution we seek to know ourselves and our world from the tiniest form on this planet to the very birth of our universe. The giant step from consciousness that orders all evolution of life to the next higher order of consciousness known as Symbolic Consciousness where consciousness becomes self-aware. Language, writing with symbols, art, music and science itself are all higher orders of Symbolic Consciousness. To me, gemstones and minerals are that primordial natural symbol as part of this Earth that inspires us to create and be that beacon of light to ourselves and others.

The Archetypal World of the Mineral Kingdom – The Science of Crystallography and the Nature of Consciousness

For centuries our view of sacred geometry has been focused and defined by the five platonic forms found in nature. These five forms have represented the ideal geometry found in the symmetry of life seeking perfection. But in nature, as seen in the mineral kingdom, there are Seven Crystal Systems that define greater and greater levels of symmetry. From science we now know the five plutonic forms, defined by Plato back so many centuries ago, are the symmetry of only one of these Seven Systems of Symmetry. All five plutonic forms are forms within just the Isometric System - which we now know as one of the seven. Plato got it right in that they are the idealized most symmetrical forms found in nature. But this leaves life static and not a process that is hidden in a clue in the other six systems.

Our knowledge of consciousness has been limited to our awareness of the sacred. Since the 19th century scientists have begun to uncover the hidden secrets of the atom and changed our view of reality from Newtonian physics to Quantum physics, confirming what metaphysicians and mystics have been saying all along. Which is: all life in all its forms, is seeking that ideal state called perfection. In science it is defined as suspended animation or Zero Degrees Kelvin. In the mineral kingdom you can see nature seeking its highest state of symmetry and perfection. This seeking of perfection is the very drive of an atom and the very drive of our consciousness. We as conscious beings, direct our thoughts and feelings every moment of our life towards this aim. From quantum physics we know form follows thought, as consciousness is reflected by geometry. Function precedes all form. Your very thoughts or brilliant ideas come long before you manifest them into reality as a physical form. From chaos to harmony the rhythms and patterns of the universe is in constant motion. From chaos all forms of life seek the most stable state of rest. The one principle of harmony drives every form from crystals to humans to seek the most stable state of perfection. The ideal state is never reached by the universe, but continues to define and expand greater and greater levels of complexity.

Consciousness first crystallized on the Earth plane through

geometry of atoms and molecules in the form of crystals and minerals. The archetypal nature of consciousness was encoded and frozen for all time in the mineral kingdom. Working with crystals is a powerful tool because it connects us immediately to our spiritual ancestry. The geometric shapes of the mineral kingdom can ground us to the Earth plane and helps us reflects back to us the steps in all processes that unfold and expand in our universe. By understanding and then knowing the Seven Crystal Systems we can expand our awareness of how consciousness works as well as giving us a metaphysical tool to reflect a grander awareness of ourselves, others and life as we understand it.

In the mineral kingdom you can see nature seeking its highest state of symmetry and perfection. The unique combination of elements joining in a union seeking the most stable state on the physical can be individual minerals' crystal system of symmetry. Holding a diamond crystal that has formed into a perfect watery transparent octahedron, one cannot help but fathom the intelligence that went into forming it. The physical properties like durability and brilliance become principles we have made archetypal to our lives. Reflected throughout human culture one can see principles emulating Nature's drive towards perfection. A perfect example of this is a core principle of the United States of America, taken from the first sentence of the constitution, "We the People of the United States, in order to form a more perfect Union,…" This core principle drives our nation. The Seven Crystal System of Consciousness can act as a powerful tool that serves as a key to our stellar ancestry and a doorway to engage metaphysics in creating our reality on the physical plane. Creating by generating positive ideas that have lasting impact in our world.

We know as individuals that the world means many different things to many different people. It is from where you stand on this Earth that the world takes on meaning to us individually. I have learned through many travels to foreign and remote parts of the world how diverse life can grow and evolve. The point here is that one must begin by picking a point, an initial place of reference. That reference will change from day to day, year to year but having a reference gives one a point to view from. This is true in the way we have defined crystallography and its uncanny symmetry and also true how we make judgement calls throughout our lives. It is a point of reference.

What was earlier presnted to you in the preceeding pages was a point of reference. A beginning to where the possibilities are endless. This point is based within the very chemistry of the Earth and the uncanny intelligence via the physics of the geometry of crystals.

It is in this chapter I intended to introduce the beginning of the blending and the synergy of the science of crystals and the metaphysics of consciousness. It can be seen as a tool for probing one's inner nature. A tool whereby one may investigate one's sub and unconscious mind. The intelligence of the crystal world can be seen as a symbolic map of consciousness. It is through the knowledge and understanding of the world of crystals and the mineral kingdom where an individual with interest will find many answers to questions of a deeper nature. Like all tools, it is not the answer itself or the only tool, but one means of self-discovery and reflection. These tools happened just to be Earth-borne and based, and not just created by humanity's inner intelligence like the enneagram, tarot, numerology, I Ching or even astrology.

The Seven Crystal System of minerals is a frozen record of life seeking perfection and reaching states excellence. What a perfect mirror for us to reflect and contemplate upon. If you believe in the Law of Attraction, then our love for gemstones runs deeper than just the beauty we see.

Like the I Ching or Tarot you have the oracle itself, then the interpretation. Be conscious of the differences. This is also true of what I'm presenting here. The real unique difference here is that Transformational Crystallography is an earth-based oracle defined on the science we know, whereas other oracles like those mentioned above are devised by man. I am presenting the grid or network seen as the Seven Crystal Systems as defined by science, then connecting this to the metaphysical concept that all form is created by the creative thought process. How I have interpreted this stems from my own study and exploration of the science of crystals, the knowledge and study of archetypal and cross cultural symbols, along with my own experience and study of consciousness. Over the decades in working in and studying the field of gemology/mineralogy, I began to see similarities between the different personality types and the gemstones that they were attracted to. This is where I first began to believe that there is a direct connection between the geometry of crystals and the power of creative thought.

It has been said in many metaphysical treaties that as we as consciences began our descent from Higher Consciousness, it was through thought and the condensing of light particles to tighter and tighter pockets of energetic resolution that we entered the first level of physicality known as the mineral kingdom. It was from this point that we were able to move on to the plant, animal, and now human kingdom. Now it seems that we have reached a new turning point in our quest. Stirring deep within us is that memory of "Home", and what better way to find our way home then to look to our beginning on this planet as a clue. It is in the seed that has already determined what type of tree it will be. It is the very first molecular relationship of atoms that determine the way the crystal will appear in physical form to our naked eye. The universe in its infinitely diverse forms has written into it that all life will seek its absolute state of motionlessness, and the way to achieve this is through joining its parts in tighter and tighter arrangements of symmetry. Symmetry is the resonant pattern of two or more objects that repeats itself in a 360¡ lattice network. It then becomes understandable that when we humans have a vision, that vision stirs many related ideas that are intimately related. Those ideas then bring on streams of thoughts and before you know it you have a complex interactive body of knowledge and information. A symmetrical network spinning from the vision at the same time trying to reach that point of vision. From wholeness evolves definition, from definition comes individuation, and with complete individuation, the wholeness can be experienced.

APPENDIX

Lazaris

For Further Information on Lazaris material:

www.lazaris.com

In the USA: 1-800-678-2356
Overseas: 1-407-401-8990

E-mail: conceptsynergy@lazaris.com

Angeles Arrien

For further information on the late Angeles Arrien's material and books, start at:

www.angelesarrien.com

BIBLIOGRAPHY

Awards

NICHE Award Winner 1991
"Maine Phoenix" Maine Tourmaline of watermelon, red and Green 179cts, .52ct trillion Diamond and 18k yellow gold

AGTA 1991
Spectrum Award Winner - 3rd Place
Opal 42cts, Chrysoprase, Black Jade, Rainbow Labradorite, Diamonds and 18k yellow gold. Hand woven 18k yellow gold chain

AGTA 1991
Cutting Edge Award Winner - 3rd Place
Arizona Gem Silica Chrysocolla Carving 39.60cts. Carving category

AGTA 1995
Cutting Edge Award Winner - 2nd Place
Arizona Botryoidal Silicated Chrysocolla and Malachite Carving 75.09cts

AGTA 1996
Cutting Edge Award Winner - Honorable Mention
Mojave Blue Chalcedony Carving 337.20cts. Carving category

AGTA 1996
Cutting Edge Award Winner - Honorable Mention
Uvarovite Drusy and Black Agate Set 368.62cts. Pairs and
suites category

AGTA 1996
Cutting Edge Award Winner - 3rd Place
Citrine TorusRing Cut 21.84cts. Combination Category

**Idar-Oberstein, Germany Carvers and Engravers Award
1996**
Montana Golden Sapphire TorusRing 4.02cts, African Blue
Chalcedony Carving 82.16cts, Black Drusy Agate Carving
Set 124.49cts. DM 500 Prize Honorable Mention. One of two
foreign entries to win for the first time the German Carvers
and Engravers Association Award.

AGTA 1998
Cutting Edge Award Winner - 1st Place
Montana Golden Sapphire TorusRing 4.02cts, African Blue
Chalcedony Carving 82.16cts, Black Drusy Agate Carving
Set 124.49cts. First place in Carving Category

AGTA 2003
Cutting Edge Award Winner - 1st Place
Carving of 226cts Chrysocolla

AGTA 2005
Cutting Edge Award Winner - 1st Place
Carving of 194cts Aquamarine

AGTA 2009
Cutting Edge Award Winner - 2nd Place
Carving of 70cts Orange Transparent Opal

AGTA 2016
Cutting Edge Award Winner - Honorable Mention
Gem Silica Chrysocolla 53.57cts Carving

AGTA 2016
Cutting Edge Award Winner - 2nd Place
Lightning Ridge Black Opal 48.46cts Carving

AGTA 2017
Cutting Edge Award Winner - Honorable Mention
Danburite 30.37cts and Burmese Ruby 1.03cts KaleidosCut

Magazine Covers

AJM, American Jewelry Magazine, October 1990
Lapidary Journal, June 1995
Lapidary Journal, June 1996
Lapidary Journal, January 1996
Lapidary Journal, February 1996
Colored Stone, March/April 1996
Professional Jeweler, December 1999
Lapidary Journal, May 2000
The Basel Magazine, May 2000
California Geology, July/August 2000
Tucson Buyer Guide, Lapidary Journal 2000
AJM, American Jewelry Magazine, January 2001
Lizzadro Museum 40th Anniversary Museum Cover, 2002
Gems and Gemology, Spring 2005

Museum Exhibitions

Carnegie Museum, Pittsburgh, PA
Los Angeles County Museum of Natural History, L.A., CA
Gemological Institute of America, Carlsbad, CA
Lizzadro Museum of Lapidary Art, Chicago, Il
Smithsonian Institute, Washington, D.C.
Ferstman Institute, Academy of Science, Moscow, Russia
Oberstein Museum, Idar-Oberstein, Germany
The Hermitage, St. Petersburg, Russia

Television Appearances

Travel Channel: Cash and Treasures - Benitoite
HSH: Guest Host - 2008-09
Gemporia UK, USA and India: Guest host and selling Lehrer
Branded Gemstones and Jewelry - 2011-present
Oprah Winfrey Show: On The New Age - 1987 (chapter 13)

Books

Adrienne, C, (1998) The Purpose of Your Life: Finding
Your Place in the World Using Synchronicity, Intuition, And
Uncommon Sense - 1998, profile on Mr. Lehrer, version 1.

Bennett, Steve (2011) The Lure of Gems, An Encyclopaedic
Guide Volume 1. Colored Plate, 218. Forward written by
Lehrer, on Glenn Lehrer page 473.

Federman, D. (1992) Modern Jeweler's Gem Profile/2: The
Second 60. Colored Plate, 100.

Matlins, A. (2001). Colored Gemstones: The Antoinette Matlins Buying Guide – How to Select, Buy, Care For & Enjoy Sapphires, Emeralds, Rubies and Other Colored Gems with Confidence and Knowledge. Woodstock: GemStone Press.

Newman, R. (1997). Gemstone Buying Guide. Colored Plates, 24, 25, 29, 57, 91.

Newman, R. (2000). Ruby, Sapphire & Emerald Buying Guide, 2000, Colored Plates, 35, 56, 88.: International Jewelry Publications, Los Angeles, California, USA.

Newman, R. (2000).Gold and Platinum Buying and Guide, 2000, Colored Plate, 28.

Newman, R. (2001). Gemstone Buying Guide, 2001, Colored Plates, 28.

Newman, R. (2011). Exotic Gems Volume 2, 2011, Colored Plates, 86.

Newman, R. (2012). Rare Gemstones, 2011, Colored Plates, 28, 30, 31.

Newman, R. (2016). Gemstone Buying Guide, 2016, Colored Plates, 13, 25, 50, 77, 87, 121.

Sinkankas, J. (1997), Gemstones of North America, Vol.III. Colored Plate, 10.

Wise, R. (2006). Secrets of the Gem Trade. The Connoisseur's Guide to Precious Gemstones. Massechusetts: Brunswick House Press - one of four gem artist profiled in book, 114.

Feature Articles

Clark, S. (1995). Carats and Characters. In Illumination. Fall/ Winter, 3, 6.

Edwards, M. (2001). Larkspur Jewelry Design Firm is a Real Gem. In Marin Journal. April, 4.

Frazier, A. & Frazier, S. (1990). Phoenix. In Lapidary Journal December, 38-52.

Frazier, A. and Frazier, S. (1993). Designing with Drusy. In Lapidary Journal. Sept, 24-27, 98, 100, 102, 104.

Frazier, A. and Frazier, S. (1993). Swords of Peace. In Lapidary Journal. December, 26-28, 90-91.

Frazier, A. and Frazier, S. (1996). Idar Meets California. In Lapidary Journal. February, 16-21.

Jeffrey, S. (1989). The Sacred Heart Crystal. In Crystal Pathways. 5 .

Kammerling, R.C. & Koivula, J.I. (1990). Large Topaz Sculpture. In Gems & Gemology. Winter, 306.

Lehrer, G. (2000). Setting a Stone Inside the Torus. Lapidary Journal. May, 251-254.

McCarthy, C. (1995/6). Gem Carving American Style. In Gem Magazine, 46-48.

McCarthy, C. (1996). Bird is the Word. In Lapidary Journal. January, 26-31.

McKenna, T.J. (2001). Glenn Lehrer Shapes Splendid Gems. In The Loupe, GIA World News. Summer, 5.

Pesheck. L. (2000). The Best of Both Worlds. In JQ Magazine. May, 162-171.

Shor, R. (1996) Glenn Lehrer's Torus Rings: Fantasy Cuts for a Bigger Market. In JCK. February.

Wade, S. (2001).Gem of an Idea. In Lapidary Journal. January, 18-19.

Webb, D. (1988). The Empress of Lemuria. In Lapidary Journal. June, 38-40.

Webb, D. (1992). The Evolution of Crystal Power. Interview with David Webb. In New Age Retailer. September, 50-60.

Weldon, R. (1999). A Lovely Apparition—Angel emerges from two of the industry's creative souls. In Professional Jeweler. December 1999, cover, and 72.

Wheaton, H.L. (2000). Circles of Light. In Lapidary Journal. May, 224-229.

White, M. (1995). Melting into Flight. In Lapidary Journal. June, 18-26.

(2001). US Gemstone Designer Ventures into Asia with Unique Cut. In Jewellery New Asia. September, 198.

(2001). A Match Made in Heaven-Mark Schneider and Glenn Lehrer," In AJM. June, 60, 62.

(1990). JA's New Designers for 1990. In JCK. August, 326.

Multi-faceted show sure to please gem lovers. In The Daily Review, pg. C11 .

"Setting it Straight," Ginger Dick, AJM, Aug. 1992. Pgs.12-16.

Upper Cuts Ginger Dick . In American Jewelry Manufacturer. October, 77-80 .

(1992). Out of the Clear Blue. In Jewel Siam. March/April, 65-67.

(1991). Spectrum Awards. In GZ European Jeweler. April, 123.

(2000). Working Together Facets . In Lapidary Journal. March, 10.

(2000). Giant Beauty. In Colored Stone. March/April, 8.

(2000). It's A Gem. In Departures. October, 129.

Teaching and Lectures

Lehrer, G. (2001). Gemstone Cuts for the New Millennium. At the International Colored Stone Association Conference. Australia.

Lehrer, G. (2001). On Gem Carving and the Art. San Diego Jewelry and Gemstone Society and G.I.A., May

Lehrer, G. (1999). Los Angeles County Museum Counsel, at the LA county Museum of Natural History

Lehrer, G. GIA Student Body, Santa Monica, CA, 1995, 96, 97, 98, 2001, 2003 on The Art of Gem Carving

Lehrer, G. (1997). JCK. At the Orlando Jewelry Trade Show .

Lehrer, G. (1994). AGTA. At the Gem and Mineral Show. Tucson, AZ , 95,96,97,98.

Lehrer, G. (1997) Institute of Noetic Sciences, Sausalito, CA, 1997, The Geometry and Color of Consciousness—A Metaphysical and Gemological Perspective

Lehrer, G. (1997) Lehrer Designs Gallery, Larkspur, CA, 2000, The Geometry and Color of Consciousness—A Metaphysical and Gemological Perspective

Lehrer, G. On Lehrer's Art. GIA Alumni and Gems and Mineral Societies: California, New York, Washington D.C .

Member of Organizations

American Gem Trade Association: Firm member.
Has served on the board of directors for 8 years.

International Colored Stone Association.

Colourful Life Foundation.
Currently serving as a trustee on the board.